FISHING IN NORTHERN CALIFORNIA

THE COMPLETE GUIDE

Ken Albert

MARKETSCOPE Box 171, Aptos, CA 95001
(408) 688-7535

ISBN 0-934061-00-9

Cover Design: Electric Art Studios
                Mountain View, CA

Printed by: Delta Lithograph
              Van Nuys, CA

This book is dedicated to Carol, my wife
and best friend for the last 26 years.
Hey, Carol, how about we do something
really important for a change? Let's
pledge to go fishing more often!

Fishing is a chance to wash one's soul with
pure air. It brings meekness and inspiration,
reduces our egotism, soothes our troubles and
shames our wickedness. It is discipline in
the equality of men - for all men are equal
before fish.

Herbert Hoover

Acknowledgements

First, a sincere and heartfelt thanks to the many fine outdoor writers, editors and publishers in Northern California. Their support and encouragement was most welcome. A personal thanks to Diane Dirksen and Bob Reeves, the creators and publishers of Recreational Lakes of California, for their advice and encouragement. A special thanks to Neil Wilkinson, at Delta Lithographers for his caring efforts. Thank you to Spiros Bairaktaris of Electirc Art Studios for a great cover design. And, finally, thanks to all the fishing experts who unselfishly shared their local fishin-hole knowledge.

Order Form

To: Marketscope
     P.O. Box 171
     Aptos, CA 95001

FISHING IN NORTHERN CALIFORNIA . . . $12.95
Sales Tax 85
Postage & Handling 1.10
Check Enclosed $14.90

Send To: Name_____
          Address_____

          _____

Order Form

To: Marketscope
     P.O. Box 171
     Aptos, CA 95001

FISHING IN NORTHERN CALIFORNIA . . . $12.95
Sales Tax 85
Postage & Handling 1.10
Check Enclosed $14.90

Send To: Name_____
          Address_____

          _____

Contents

Contents(contd)

Great Fishing

Fishing is great in Northern California. There are 5,000 lakes and 30,000 miles of streams in California, and the vast majority of these lakes and streams are in Northern California. And then there are the hundreds of miles of coastline, San Francisco Bay and 700 miles of waterways in the Delta. Anglers here are fortunate to have an immense variety of quality fishing opportunities;

- Steelhead and salmon in coastal rivers.

- Rainbow and brown trout in Sierra streams.

- Striped bass, salmon, steelhead, shad and catfish in valley rivers.

- Black bass, trout, salmon, catfish and panfish in numerous lakes and resevoirs.

- Striped bass, sturgeon and halibut in Bay waters.

- Salmon, albacore, rockfish and lingcod in the Pacific.

And most of this great fishing is accessible, quite simple, and requires only modestly priced tackle. An added benefit, fishing is a wonderful way to share the outdoor experience with the entire family.

But the immense variety of the Northern California fishing experiences does raise many questions. Some major, others just puzzling;

- What size hook(or line) do I use for trout(or catfish)?

- Where are the bass hotspots at Amador, or New Hogan?

- How do I catch striper in the Delta?

- If I catch a halibut(or a catfish, or a ...), how do I clean it?

- When is the hot halibut season in San Franciso Bay?

- What is a spinnerbait?

- Can I fish from shore at San Pablo Reservoir?

- Where are the best spots to fish along the Sacramento River?

- How do I clean and cook a sturgeon?

- Can I rent a boat(or camp) at New Melones?

- What are the surest producers for largemouth bass?

- What rod and reel do I need for steelhead?

- When is the best time to go on an albacore trip?

Fishing In Northern California answers all these questions and many, many more. For all of the types of fish and different locations, it tells;

- How to fish?

- Where to fish?

- When to fish?

- What equipment, tackle, rigs, bait and lures to use?

- How to clean and preserve your catch?

- How to cook each fish?

Take a Kid Fishing - One Story

My thirteen year old son, Bruce, had been after me for months to go fishing with him in tiny Freedom Lake, about four miles from our home. He'd heard at school that kids had caught some nice bass there. So late one Saturday afternoon, we loaded our row boat into the pick-up and drove to the lake.

I took my big, old, metal tackle box. It had been my father's box. He had it packed with bass plugs, bucktails, even live-frog harnesses. Everything that was "state of the art" in the 1930's. For some reason, my dad, gave up bass fishing before I was born. Oh, he took us fishing, and my brother and I loved it, but never did he take us bass fishing. He was killed in an industrial accident when I was a teenager. I inherited his love for fishing and his big, metal tackle box.

All the lures that my father used 40 and 50 years ago to entice the lunker bass are still in that metal tackle box, but I've added others, including the "big two" of modern bass fishing - spinnerbait and plastic worms. Actually, I hardly ever use any of his lures, since they're almost antiques and I don't want to lose them. Besides, I score most with spinnerbait and plastic worms. This is what Bruce and I were tossing at Lake Freedom. We tossed and we tossed and we tossed and we were getting skunked. The sun had set and I was ready to go home for dinner.

For some reason, Bruce looked into his grandfather's tackle box, spotted an old red bucktail with three small fish shaped flashers that protected the hook. "Dad, why don't you try this? It's sort of like a spinnerbait, isn't it?" he said.

"Yea, I guess it is", I responded, as I continued to work my worm.

"Come on, try it. Let's see how it swims".

"O.K., we'll give it a try".

I decided to humor him, so I snapped it on and pulled it beside the boat to watch the action. "It looks pretty good. Like a spinnerbait", I said. Bruce agreed.

My first cast with this well-built, old relic landed
near some overhanging branches, about 8 feet from shore.
When I began my retrieve, the line stiffened and my rod
arched. "Damn, I've snagged an underwater branch," I said
under my breath. I was upset. I didn't want to lose that
lure. For some reason, I didn't want to lose anything from
that old, metal box.

But, then the snag began to "run" and take line against
my drag. What do you know, I had a strike on the first cast
of a lure that hadn't been in the water since before World
War II.

We landed the bass. It was a beauty. Bruce couldn't
resist the temptation to say, "See, Dad, I told you so.
Those old lures are good." "They sure are," I grinned.

Then we agreed that the fish should be released. Lake
Freedom needed that bass, and we needed to know that it was
alive and well. After all, it and that old lure performed
a minor miracle. It was that old lure that gave Bruce and
I a wonderful moment together. That old lure made me cherish
my father's tackle box even more. And, it tied together a
grandfather and grandson who never knew each other, except
for a few moments at Lake Freedom.

Bruce switched to one of his grandfather's spinner-
bait-like lures and we each made a few more casts into the
twilight. Then Bruce said, "Dad, let's go home. I don't
want to risk losing this lure. We can't see the overhanging
branches." I noded, and we rowed to shore. During the drive
home, Bruce chattered about how to tell Mom our fishing story
and how to convince her with no fish as proof. But, I was
thinking about something else. I was thinking that someday
Bruce would be a loving keeper of that big metal tackle box
and those old lures.

Fishing Tips

There is one element of fishing success that can't be taught or learned. Rather, it must be self-instilled. I'm talking about self-confidence. Often "how-to" fishing articles end with a pep talk on the importance of fishing with confidence - that old Positive Mental Attitude. You know it's corny, but somehow it works.

I personally feel so strongly about the need to have faith in your approach and your tackle, that I'm going to reverse things and put this topic first. I love fishing even when I don't catch fish. But, I love it even more when I do. Often the only difference between an angler who puts fish on the line and one who just wets his line, is attitude. So, fish with confidence.

Confidence will make you more attentive and more aware. It keeps your mind in gear. But, most importantly, it will encourage you to experiment, to change baits, or lures, or depths, or location, until you find fish. This book tells you all you need to know to catch any kind of fish in Northern California. Just add self-confidence.

When to Fish

There is no question that the time of year, the time of month and the time of day all impact on fishing success. More so, for some species, than others. All life moves in cycles. Fish are no different. For example, it's no coincidence, that most of California's fishing records were set in the spring months. March, April and May are probably the best months to fish. These are the spawning months. Simply stated, here are the best times to fish;

1. <u>Time Of Year</u>

Spring is best all around, followed by fall. Winter is surprisingly good. Summer, for many species is the worst (yes, I know about summer vacations; the weather is beautiful and fishing seems to be a natural, warm weather sport, but often the fish don't know this. Or maybe they do!). However, some fishing is good in summertime, especially if the proper approaches are followed. On the next page is a table that highlights the best time of year to fish for each species. It's easy to see why fishing is a four season sport in Northern California.

2. Time Of Day

For most types of fish, during most times of the year, there is little doubt that early morning(from first light until 8-9 am) and late evening(the 2-3 hours before dark) are the best times of day to catch fish. These are the times of day when fish are active and feeding. For some situations night time is also good. For example, bass fishing after dark on warm summer nights, using noisy, dark surface plugs (in shallow water) can be good. Also, summertime catfishing can be good from 9-12 pm and during the two hours before daybreak.

3. Time Of Month(The Tides)

Some would say that the phases of the moon have a great deal to do with fishing success, in any environment. This may or may not be true. But, there is no doubt that tides do impact fishing success in shallower tidal waters, especially the San Francisco Bay and the Delta. In these locations, it's always best to fish on days when there is a big change between high and low tide. Waters move faster, bait and bait fish get moved around, so game fish feed more actively.

The height of the tide varies according to the positions of the sun and moon in relation to the earth. These influences are illustrated below. The best fishing is during spring tide periods. Fish the hours before, through and after a high tide change for peak action.

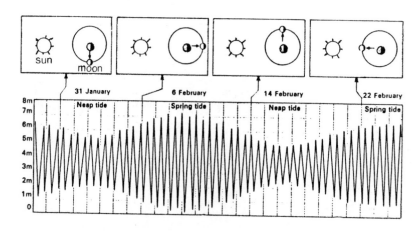

Best Time to Fish

Fishing Seasons   (+=good, -=fair)

Species	J	F	M	A	M	J	J	A	S	O	N	D
Abalone				-	-	-		+	+	-	-	
Albacore								-	+	-		
Bass		-	+	+	+	-	-	-	-	+	-	
Catfish		-	-	-	-	-	+	+	+	-	-	
Halibut							-	+	+	-		
Kokanee		-	-	+	+	+	+	-	-			
Lingcod	+	+	-	-	-	-	-	-	-	+	+	+
Rock Cod	-	-	-	-	-	-	-	-	-	-	-	-
Salmon												
-Ocean		-	-		+	+		-	-	-		
-S.F. Bay								-	-	-		
-Rivers							-	+	+	+	+	-
-Lakes	+	+	+	+	-	-	-	-	-	-	+	+
Shad				-	+	+	-					
Sharks	-	-	-	-	-	-	-	-	-	-	-	-
Steelhead	+	+	+	-				-	-	+	+	+
Striped Bass												
-Ocean							-	+	+	-	-	
-Bays			-	-	-	-	-	+	+	+	+	-
-Rivers	+	+	+	-	-	-			-	-	+	+
Sturgeon												
-Bays	+	+	+	-	-	-	-	-	-	-	+	+
-Rivers	+	+	-	-	-	-	-	-	-	-	-	+
Trout												
-Streams				+	+	+	-	-	+	+	+	
-Lakes	+	+	+	+	-	-	-	-	-	-	+	+

Where to Fish

This book has tons of "where to fish" information in it. But there are three generalizations about "where to fish" that apply so universally, that they are worthy of special note.

1. <u>Fish On The Bottom!</u>

To catch many varieties of Northern California fish you've got to fish on or near the bottom. This is true for;

- Bass — even in deep water they're usually near structures.

- Catfish

- Crayfish

- Halibut

- Lingcod

- Rock Cod

- Rockcrabs

- Salmon(in rivers)

- Steelhead

- Striped bass

- Sturgeon

- Trout — Stream trout will rise up for food, but then retreat to the bottom. Trout near shore in lakes, are on the bottom.

I'd like to empahsize the truism, "fish on the bottom" with this analogy. Most creatures that live on land, actually live on the bottom of a vast sea of atmosphere. This atmosphere is about 100,000 feet deep, yet most creatures live right on the bottom of the atmosphere. Of course, people and all fur bearing animals live on the bottom, but so do most birds and insects. Birds and insects spend most of their time in and around the ground, plants and trees that are part of the atmospheres bottom structure. Well, the same is true of most fish. Water is their atmosphere. And the bottom of the water is their land. It provides food, shelter and security.

The primary Northern California game fish that are consistently caught in open water(not near the bottom) are salmon(in the ocean), albacore, kokanee(a land locked salmon), trout and some sharks.

2. Fish At The Right Water Temperature

In big Northern California lakes and resevoirs, the key factor in finding fish during the summer months is water temperature. Lakes stratify into three distinct layers with the coming of summer and stay that way until fall. The middle layer of water, called the thermocline, has a large concentration of dissolved oxygen, baitfish and therefore, trout and salmon. The thermocline, which provides the right temperature for trout and salmon metabolism, is down from 10 to 80 feet, depending on season and lake characteristics.

LAKE STRATIFICATION
Surface

Epilimnion Layer

Thermocline Layer
Oxygen and Baitfish Rich

Hypolimnion Layer

Bottom

Gauges for measuring water temperatures at various depths are available for as little as $5-10. On the next page are the temperatures where you are likely to find fish.

Species	Optimum Temperature	Temperature Range
Salmon	55°	44–58°
Lake trout	50	43–53
Brown & rainbow trout	55–60	44–75
Striped bass	70–72	60–78
Bass, largemouth	70–72	–
smallmouth	64–66	–
Panfish	64–66	–

3. Fish Don't Like Direct Light

This is one reason why fishing drops off when the morning sun hits a lake. But, there are things you can do. For instance, if you're catching fish in a lake early in the day, try deeper down as the light increases. Or, if you're fishing a trout stream, work the shady side. This also applies to lake shores.

Playing and Landing

A variety of fishing techniques are needed to entice a fish to bite or strike. Once this is accomplished, whether you've got a bass or a sturgeon on the other end of your line, there is a certain commonality in playing a larger fish. Here are the elements;

1. Pull the rod up and back forcefully to set the hook. Don't be tentative. Hold the reel handle firmly, so no line is given. After setting, adjust the drag, if necessary.

2. Hold the rod tip up when playing a fish. The rod butt should be held against the stomach area. Lower the rod tip and reel in, simultaneously. Pump the rod upwards to move the fish in. Then,

again reel in on the down stroke. This rod "pumping" allows you to reel in when tension on the line and terminal tackle is not at its maximum.

3. Never give a fish slack. If it charges, reel in fast. Try to guide fish away from your boat with rod tip high. But, if the fish does get under your boat, put the rod tip down into the water to prevent line abrasion or twisting around the outdrive.

4. If your fish runs, let him go against the drag. That's what it's for. Then, slowly bring him back by reeling in, or if necessary, using the pumping technique.

5. Keep the rod tip high while landing. This allows the rod to act as a shock absorber and prevents the chance of slack line. Net the fish from below and in front.

Catch and Release

There is a growing awareness among anglers that the fish resource is limited. And some anglers now feel that the ultimate fishing experience is not to "take a limit" but to catch and release as many fish as possible. Of course, no one should keep more fish than they can use, or keep a fish that they don't enjoy eating.

Obviously, catch and release is a personal decision. It's also a practice that can be and should be exercised on a selective basis. Sometimes a fish shouldn't be re- leased - for example, a badly hooked, bleeding fish, or a small rockfish that has been brought up from 50 fathoms, and is dead on arrival. For some reason, I personally don't like to take fish that are about to spawn. I know this is somewhat irrational since it's absolutely true that whenever in a fishes lifecycle, you take it, you're forever preventing that fish from spawning. But I guess I just feel that when a fish has made it through all the hurdles and survived all the predators and all the hazards, that it has a right to spawn without me interferring. On the other hand, I don't mind taking fish that are in abundant supply or even those that are planted regularly.

When you do want to release fish, there are several things you can do to improve the chances for the fish;

1. Use barbless hooks(or flatten down barbs with a pliers).

2. Avoid fishing with bait, if possible, and if you do use bait, don't use a sliding sinker rig. Hookings with sliding sinker rigs are often very deep.

3. Use a needlenose pliers to remove hooks(see special instructions for salmon release in Catching Salmon In The Ocean).

4. Hold the unhooked fish in a swimming position in the water and quickly move it forward repeatedly, to force water through its gills. Do this until the fish revives enough to struggle and swim out of your hands.

Rods and Reels

How-to-catch each of the major sports fishes in Northern California is described in detail in this book. There are 19 of them in all. Rod and reel recommendations are made in each section. But, not only are the most desirable rod and reel combinations noted, but so are alternatives that often work just as well. So happily, you don't need 19 rod and reel sets to enjoy all the fishing experiences in this book.

Often, one rod and reel is useful in several types of fishing. For example, a boat rod and conventional saltwater-sized reel can be used for salmon trolling, striper trolling, sturgeon, halibut, lingcod and rock cod. This may even be over kill in some situations, since a lightweight spinning outfit can be used to troll or cast for average striper(6-10pounds). This same light spinning outfit can be used for trout(both lake and stream), bass casting, panfishing, even steelhead in smaller coastal streams. In fact, an angler doesn't even need a fly rod and reel to fly fish, but don't tell avid fly anglers this.

A casting bobber on spinning equipment will deliver a fly. See Catching Trout(in streams). And talking about stream trout fishing, one hot item now is the mini-spinning out-fit - a 5 foot rod and tiny reel. It's fun to use but spinners can also usually be delivered effectively using a 7 foot rod and normal sized reel filled with 4 pound test line.

Fortunately, rods and reels of good quality(not gold-plated, but good quality) are not that expensive. But, before considering a specialized rod and reel, first consider using what you've got on hand. Look at what others are using when you get to the water. I'm always surprised at the variety. Besides, the fish doesn't know what's on the other end of the line. Good line, tied well, a decent drag and know how will land most fish.

Knots and Hooks

A good fishing knot is one that stays tied and one that doesn't weaken the line too much. There are many knots that fit these criteria, but most veteran anglers use only one or two basic knots. The best overall knot is probably the improved clinch knot. It can be used to tie hooks to leaders, swivels to line, etc. There are two versions;

An often neglected item is the fishing hook. It's important to keep them sharp. Inexpensive little sharp-ners are made just for this purpose. Both bait hooks and lure hooks get abused, in use, and in tackle boxes, so do sharpen them up, regularly.

The designation system used in fishing hook sizing can be confusing for those who don't deal with it regularly.

- large hooks(1/0 and up) increase in size as the number increases. (So a 4/0 is a larger hook than a 2/0).

- Small hooks(1 and down) decrease in size as the number increases. (So a 6 is a larger hook than a 10).

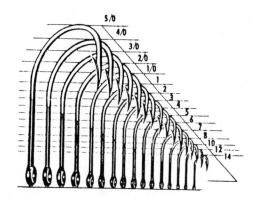

A leading hook manufacturer(Eagle Claw) makes the following hook size recommendations;

- Panfish: Bluegill - 8 down to 12
            Crappie - 4

- Bass: smallmouth - 3/0 down to 4
         largemouth - 8/0 down to 4
         striped   - 3/0 up to 10/0

- Catfish: up to 5# - 4 down to 12
            large   - 4 up to 8/0

- Trout: rainbow   - 5 down to 14
          brown   - 5 down to 14
          steelhead - 2 up to 6/0

- Salmon   - about 6/0

Chart Recorder

A chart recording sonar(either paper or video) is the eyes and ears of any angler operating from a boat. This device prints out a profile of the shape of the bottom and the shadows of bait schools and individual large fish. Actually, the flasher-type depth sounder provides the same information, but this equipment requires more experience and judgment to use effectively. Chart recorders are very helpful in both saltwater and bay bottom fishing for rock cod, lingcod, striper and sturgeon and for freshwater bass and trout fishing. There's little doubt that the proper use of a boat mounted chart recorder gives the angler an edge - it allows him to "almost" see the fish.

Maps

First, let me emphasize that none of the maps included in this book(or in any fishing book, for that matter) are to be used for navigational purposes. Their only intent is to indicate where the fish can be found. Navigational maps for coastal and bay waters are available at marine and boating stores. These are published by The National Oceanic and Atmospheric Administration(U.S. Department of Commerce).

There are other good maps that are especially useful to anglers;

- . U.S. Forest Service Maps - especially useful in determining which land is publicly owned.

- . U.S. Geological Survey - good for detailed topographical features, and for locating out-of-the-way fishing spots.

- . U.S. Bureau of Land Management - for streams and lakes in this agency's jurisdiction.

- . Park Scenic Maps - both federal and state parks publish maps that can be quite helpful.

- . Recreational Lakes of California - a book of lakes with maps and facilities.

- . Hal Shell's Delta Map - comprehensive map of the entire Delta waterways including facilities.

Regulations

Fishing regulations in California are simple and straightforward, but they are also detailed and specific. A Fish and Game Commission publication, "California Sport Fishing Regulations, A Summary" is available free at any location where fishing licenses are sold. This is a fact filled, well-organized brochure that has all you need to know about current regulations. Read it over and know the rules. I'm always bothered when I see a young child on a camping trip unknowingly violating regulations that are designed to protect the young fish. A stringer full of 10-12" dead stripers caught in the Delta in July is not the youngsters fault, but their uninformed parents. Specific regulations are on page 128.

California Angling Records

Athletes always say "records are made to be broken." Maybe that's still true of fishing records, too. Eighty percent(or 21 out of 26) of the records listed on the next page were set in the 1970's and 1980's! Seven were set since January 1980!

Organizations and Publications

Some of the most active fishing organizations and some of the best publications for up-to-date Northern California fishing information are;

- United Anglers of California
  1360 Neilsen Street
  Berkeley, CA 94702
  (415)-526-4049

- California Striped Bass Association
  P.O. Box 9045
  Stockton, CA 95208

- The Fish Sniffer
  P.O. Box 930
  Elkgrove, CA 95624
  (916)-685-2245

- Fishing and Hunting News
  Northern California Edition
  511 Eastlake Avenue, E
  Seattle, WA 98109
  (206)-624-2738

California Angling Records

Species	Weight (lb+oz)	Where Caught	Date
Albacore(tuna)	73-8	San Diego	Nov.82
Bass, Largemouth	21-3½	Lake Casitas	Mar.80
smallmouth	9-1	Trinity Lake	Mar.76
Catfish, blue	36-13	Lake Jennings	Aug.77
channel	41	Lake Casitas	Aug.72
flathead	55	Colorade River	Apr.80
Halibut, California	53-8	Santa Rosa Island	May 75
Kokanee	4-13	Lake Tahoe	Aug.73
Lingcod	53	Trinidad	1969
Panfish, bluegill	2-10½	Lake Los Serranos	May 76
black crappie	4-1	New Hogan Lake	Mar.75
white crappie	4-8	Clear Lake	Apr.71
Rockcod, cabezon	23-4	Los Angeles	Apr.58
Salmon, chinook	88	Sacramento River	Nov.79
coho	22	Paper Mill Creek	Jan.59
Shad, American	7-4	American River	May 82
Shark, blue	231	Santa Cruz Island	Aug.74
bonita	298-8	Anacapa Island	Jul.70
thresher	527	San Diego	Oct.80
Steelhead*	27-4	Smith River	Dec.76
Striped bass	65	San Joaquin River	May 51
Sturgeon	468	San Pablo Bay	Jul.83
Trout, brook	9-12	Silver Lake	Sep.32
brown	26-5	Lower Twin Lake	May 83
lake	37-6	Lake Tahoe	Jan.74
golden	9-8	Virginia Lake	Aug.52
Rainbow*	27-4	Smith River	Dec.76

*Rainbow and steelhead are not separated

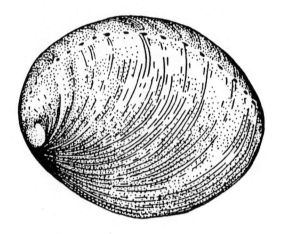

How to Catch...**Abalone**

By coincidence, this section is being prepared just one day after an abalone diver was attacked and killed by a 15 foot great white shark near Pidgeon Point(on the San Mateo county coast). Fortunately, this is not a frequent occurence. Only seven fatal shark attacks have taken place off the California-Oregon coast since records of such incidents were first kept in 1926.

Abalone is a rock-clinging, single-shelled creature that inhabits the seashore waters all along Northern California. It has a large fleshy foot and sensory projections on its underside. For most people, our closest contact with abalone is in sea shell shops and on restaurant menus (speaking of menus, abalone are delicious).

Fishing Techniques

There are three basic techniques for taking abalone;

    1. Rockpicking - searching the rocky shore on foot.

2. Free diving – diving near shore with a snorkel only(no aqualung).

3. Scuba diving – diving with an aqualung.

North of Yankee Point(at Monterey), only rockpicking
and free diving are allowed. So, scuba divers are not
permitted to take abalone anywhere along the Northern
California coast from Monterey to Bodega Bay to Fort
Bragg to Cresent City, near the Oregon border.

Rockpickers operate at low tides. Preferably a
minus low tide and a calm ocean. They start about an
hour before the low tide and quit before the incoming
tide threatens a soaking or being stranded away from
shore.

The basic technique is to comb an area looking for
abalone attached to rocks. Often it is best to feel under water in crevices and cracks that other rockpickers
have missed.

Free divers operate in the water. The wise ones in
pairs, taking turns diving down to rocky bottoms in 5-30
feet of water. Abalone are pried off the rocks with a
metal bar. Since this can fatally injure the abalone,
it is best to be sure the abalone is of legal size before
prying it off. Rockpickers must also make this judgment.
To pry the abalone off the rock and avoid injuring it,
slip the bar under the abalone. Then lift the handle
end up, pushing the tip of the bar against the rock. This
prevents injury to the abalone foot. If it is undersize,
hold the abalone back on the spot where it was taken until
it grabs hold itself.

Free diving lessons are available at selected locations along the coast. No one should attempt to free dive
without proper instruction.

Tackle and Equipment

Equipment needed for rockpicking and free diving is
listed on the next page:

- Abalone iron(of legal dimension)
- Fixed caliper measuring gauge
- State fishing license
- Catch bag(at least a gunnysack)
- Neoprene boots(optional)
- Neoprene gloves(optional)

In addition, for free diving, you'll need a wet suit, hood, snorkel, mask, fins, knife(for escaping from kelp) and a weight belt.

Where to Fish

Abalone can be found all along the Northern California coast from Monterey to the Oregon border. Good areas are scattered all along between Santa Cruz to Fort Bragg. North from Fort Bragg to Westport are the best bets. Check with dive shops and experienced abalone rockpickers and divers for more specific information.

Cleaning and Cooking

Cleaning abalone is different from most other sea food, but it is not actually difficult. Insert the abalone iron between the meat and the shell, at the pointed end of the abalone. Now, pop out the meat. Next, trim away the flanged edges and all the intestines. A pot scrubber can then be used to rub off the black skin. Scrape off the suction cups with a knife. Now it's time to tenderize the meat. Before slicing, pound it with a big mallet. Then slice it 1/8 to 1/4 inch thick. Use the mallet again for a final tenderizing. The end of a bottle may also be used for tenderizing.

Most people feel that the only way to prepare abalone is quick pan frying. Tenderized steaks are usually floured, or dipped in egg and sauteed over high heat for less than 1 minute on a side.

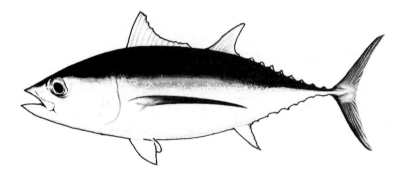

How to Catch... **Albacore**

Albacore, or long-finned tuna, often take commercial fishing boats a couple of hundred miles from shore. Commercial boats stay out until their freezers are full. Fortunately, there is a time each year when albacore come close enough to shore(35-50 miles usually), so that sport fishermen can get in on the fun. These fish migrate up the coast of California, typically hitting the waters off Monterey and San Francisco about late August. Good fishing, following their arrival, may last for as little as a week or two, or may extend for several months.

There are years when albacore fishing gets hot as close as ten miles from shore. These are the only times most sport fisherman consider albacore fishing in their own boats. At other times it's probably best to venture out on a well-equipped, fast, large party boat especially rigged for albacore. Typically the boats leave in the wee hours of the morning(about 3am) and are back in port by 7pm. Cost ranges from $50 to $75.

Fishing Techniques

Trolling is the most popular technique for taking albacore. But, before we get into trolling specifics, a word about where to troll. After all, it's a big ocean! First, albacore congregate and feed in warmer water. Most experts look for water in the 63-65° F range, with 60° F being a minimum. The second good fish finder is bird activity. Birds actively pursuing bait fish means that albacore may be doing the same thing. When birds are spotted, run the boat through the edge of the activity, not through the center. No need to chance scattering the bait fish and feeding albacore.

Albacore trolling is characterized by;

- Surface trolling relatively close to the boat, although sometimes 16 to 24 ounce torpedo sinkers are used to put the hook down somewhat.

- Fairly rapid boat speed(perhaps 8-10 knots).

- Heavy feathered albacore jigs trolled in the boat's wake. Some say 5-7 wakes out, others go out 70-100 pulls.

The other method of albacore fishing is used on party boats after a school of fish is located by trolling. The boat is stopped, and scoops of bait fish(usually anchovies) are tossed into the water to raise the albacore up to the surface. This technique is called chumming. Fishermen drift bait near the surface.

Tackle and Equipment

Albacore are big, fast, open ocean sports fish. A good fish averages 20-30 pounds, with some ranging up to 80 pounds or more.

Essential equipment includes;

- Large, iced, fish storage box(or cooler, or a plastic trash container.

. A good sized gaff.

. Medium to heavy, 6-7 foot boat rod.

. Salt water trolling or casting reel that is
  capable of holding 300 yards of 25 pound test
  monofilament line.

Lures and Bait

Feather albacore jigs.

    Description: weighted jig sold with its own leader.

    Color: red/white and green/yellow are popular.

    Size: 1-4 ounces.

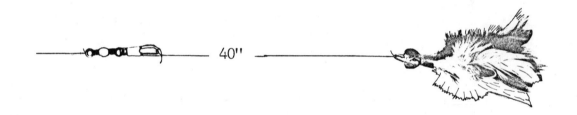

Drift bait(typically anchovies)

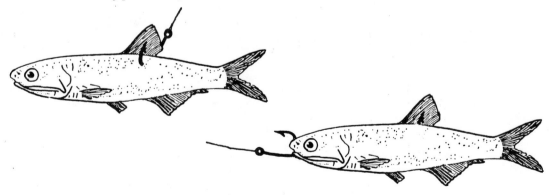

Where to Fish

It varies. But two of the better albacore grounds are Soap Run and Pioneer Sea Mount. These are both 35-55 miles out, off the coast of Davenport.

Cleaning and Cooking

Albacore is most often steaked. Make sure the dark flesh is removed from each piece.

Like salmon, albacore has a relatively high fat content. Also, like salmon, the most popular way to prepare it is barbecuing. The smoke seems to add to the flavor. Poached albacore tastes like canned tuna, but even better. Poached albacore may be stored in a refrigerator for several days, or frozen for a short time. Sauteing albacore is also popular.

LARGEMOUTH BASS

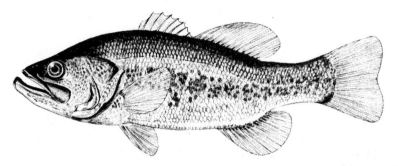

SMALLMOUTH BASS

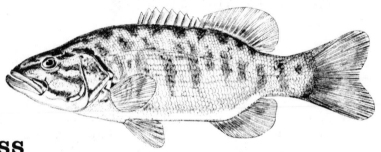

How to Catch...Bass

Largemouth bass are the most widely distributed and the most pursued black bass. They inhabit many of the resevoirs and lakes in Northern California as well as the Delta. Prime largemouth fishing grounds include Shasta, Oroville, Clear Lake, Pardee, New Hogan, etc.

Smallmouth black bass are less abundant in Northern California but can be found in selected locations. But, in truth most anglers don't care whether the bass they catch is a largemouth or a smallmouth. And why should they; most of the fishing tackle and techniques are the same, the fishing regulations and limits are the same, and both taste equally good! In reality, most Northern California black bass are largemouth, since largemouth do best in lakes and resevoirs. Smallmouth are a river oriented fish, but inhabit selected lakes.

Fishing Techniques

Bass fishing is best during the spring and fall. Ironically, probably most people fish for bass in the warm summer months. Why not? Family vacations fit best when the kids are out of school. And the weather is comfortable "out on the lake." Don't get me wrong. Bass are caught in the summer. But it takes more effort, since the fish are usually down deeper.

The basic technique used in bass fishing is casting. Still fishing and trolling are also possibilities, but are rarely used. All types of casting equipment can and is used, including bait casting, spinning, spincasting and flycasting. More on this in the Equipment/Tackle section.

Successful bass fishing centers around the answers to three questions. Where to cast? How to cast? What to cast? Here are key guidelines that will tell you where to cast in a given lake or resevoir;

- Bass are almost always on or near the bottom. The "bottom" could be near shore(say in the spring) in 2 feet of water, or it might be in 40 feet of water on the slope of a sunken island.

- Largemouth prefer to be near structures, whether it be a rocky fall-off, a sunken log, a weedbed, standing timber, a rocky point, etc. Smallmouth inhabit rocky bottoms.

- Largemouth bass prefer a water temperature of about 70° F. This means that in the spring and fall, bass are likely to be near shore, in shallow seventyish water. When the surface temperature is well above 70°, bass holding out deep make feeding forays into shallower water, primarily at night. Smallmouth prefer water in the 65-67° range.

- If you (or someone else) catches a bass at a particular spot, and the lake temperature conditions don't change, the spot will probably produce more bass.

- At an unfamiliar lake, seek information about "good spots" from other anglers, bait shops, marinas, etc.

Now on to answers to the question, "How to cast?"

  • Cast your offering so it lands near structures,
    or will be retrieved near structures. For exam-
    ple, put it next to a pile of boulders that are
    partially submerged, or right by a fallen tree.
    Retrieve parallel to a submerged log, not across
    it. Try inlets where streams flow into lakes.

  • Retrieve slowly. Seventy to eighty percent of
    the time, a slow retrieve is best. But, if it's
    not working, don't hesitate to try a rapid re-
    trieve. A combination may be in order also. For
    example, a few quick turns of the reel handle
    just after the offering lands(to get the bass's
    attention), followed by a slow retrieve.

  • Retrieve everything, except surface plugs, right
    along the bottom. Since the bass are on the bot-
    tom, you've got to put your offering on the bottom.
    Afterall, we live and eat on the "bottom" of the
    atmosphere, so doesn't it seem natural for some
    fish(particularly bass) to live and eat on the
    bottom of their "atmosphere."

  • "Feel" the bottom during your retrieve. No doubt
    this practice will result in some lost rigs, but
    it will also result in more bass. Using snagless,
    or near snagless, offerings as described later,
    will minimize loss.

  • Cast quietly. In fact, fish quietly. Minimize
    engine noise, oar lock noise, "scraping tackle
    box along the floor of the boat" noise, and so
    on. Bass fishing is akin to stalking.

The answer to the "what to cast question" is in the
lure and bait section to follow.

Tackle and Equipment

Today, many bass anglers use what is known in the trade
as a bass boat. These boats were popularized in Bass Derbys.

They are about 16-20 feet long, with pedestal seats, large outboard motors, an electric trolling motor(used for maneuvering, not trolling), several depth finders, a fish box, flashy-sparkling finish and on and on.

These boats are fun and functional, but the good news is that you don't need one to catch your share of bass. The bad news is that successful bass fishing probably does require some kind of boat that can be maneuvered along an irregular shoreline. Many kinds of boats will do, from an inflatable, to a canoe, to a dingy, to a row boat, to an aluminum boat, to a small stern drive cruiser. Shore fishing for bass is possible. I know my big brother, who was twelve at the time, caught a 5 pound bass while casting a minnow plug from a short boat dock. But, covering very much promising structures on foot is difficult.

To find promising bass territory, you'd best be equipped with maps of the lake, a thermometer that works well under water and a depth sounder(a flasher type will do).

Now, for the tackle itself. Here, there is a great deal of lattitude. The possibilties include;

- Spinning equipment - 6-7 foot, light to medium action spinning rod. Open-faced reel with 10-12 pound monofilament line.

- Spincasting equipment - 5-6 foot pistol-grip, light to medium rod. Closed-faced spinning reel with 10-12 pound monofilament line.

- Baitcasting equipment - (this is the"in" equipment). 5-6 foot pistol-grip, light to medium rod(can be used with spincasting reel). Baitcasting reel(some have magnetic anti-backlash mechanisms) with level-wind feature, star drag and 10-12 pound monofilament line.

Lures and Bait

Many an otherwise sane person is driven absolutely crazy by the immense selection of bass plugs, jigs, spoons, spinners, plastic worms, etc. And professional bass-tournament fishermen seem to own at least one of everything, based on the size of the tackle boxes in their boats!

But, don't despair. You don't need one of everything to take bass. In fact, many bass fishing experts say that one or two lures account for more bass than all the others combined. These two are 1)plastic worms and 2)spinner baits.

Plastic worms can be rigged either Texas style or Carolina style. Both are snagless(and inexpensive) so you can work them slowly along the bottom or through heavy cover without fear. Black or purple 6" floating plastic worms and No. 1 hooks are good for both rigs.

Texas Style Rig

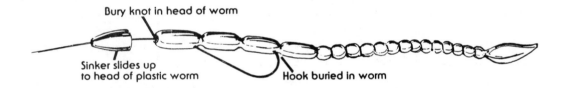

Bury knot in head of worm

Sinker slides up
to head of plastic worm

Hook buried in worm

Carolina Style Rig(one version)

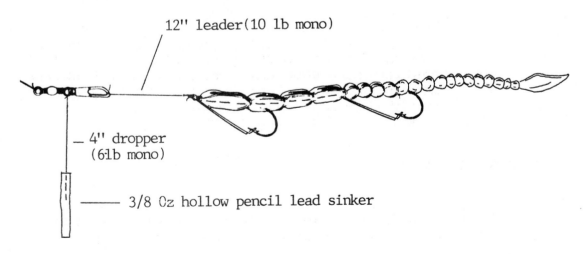

12" leader(10 lb mono)

_ 4" dropper
(6lb mono)

—— 3/8 Oz hollow pencil lead sinker

I prefer the Carolina Style because the hook point is not embedded in the worm and therefore it can be set into the bass easier. Also, the sliding swivel with weighted dropline gives the worm a freer action and you sacrifice only the sinker if you do snag-up and must pull free. The optional second hook is great for bass that take only half a worm. This rig looks complicated and expensive, but you can purchase the worm and the 2 weedless hooks already rigged in place for about $1.00. Try and find any bass plug for that price! Incidentally, for simplicity, it's possible to use the sliding bullet sinker on a Carolina Style rig (instead of the drop line).

Several typical spinnerbait styles are illustrated below;

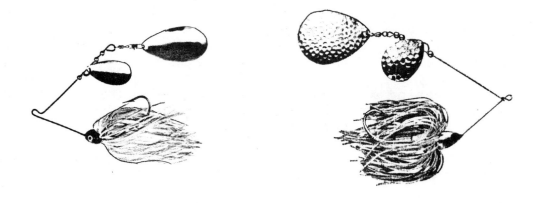

Buy several of different sizes, different numbers of spinners and different colors. Good colors are chartreuse, purple, white and yellow.

A hot tip before leaving spinnerbaits and plastic worms. Try combining them for more strikes by bigger bass. Simply put a 6 inch plastic worm on the hook of the spinner-bait. Big bass can't resist.

Compliment your plastic worm and spinnerbait collection with several top-water plugs. These are sometimes good for spring and fall fishing in shallow water. They're also good in shallow water after dark. The bass come into the shallows in the summertime to feed at night. Good lures are Nip-I-Diddee, shad imitation and crawdad imitation.

There is one more category of lure you might want to add to your arsenal. It's the skirted, leadhead jig. These have been very productive in Northern California lakes. Here's the scoop;

- Buy dark colors(like brown) in the 3/8-1/2oz. size.

- Select one with weedless hooks.

- Add a pork-rind or plastic trailer that resembles a frogs hindquarters. This is put on the hook like a piece of bait.

The jig-trailer combination is called a "pig and jig." They're usually cast out like plastic worms and then returned along the bottom. Hopping it or bouncing it along. Raise it off the bottom and let it settle.

A closing word on live bait bass fishing. It's the way the old timers did it. It works and probably produces the largest bass. But it's a lot of fuss. Artificials are so good nowadays that you really don't need the bait. If you want to try it, read up on it in one of the books in your library dedicated to black bass fishing.

Cleaning and Cooking

Bass can be scaled, gutted and beheaded. But, many prefer to fillet them. This is the easiest way to remove the scales and skin.

Bass is mild and flaky. It can be cooked in a variety of ways including sauteing, broiling, poaching, baking and frying. But, in any case, do remove the skin before cooking. Any muddy flavor is in the skin.

WHITE CATFISH

CHANNEL CATFISH

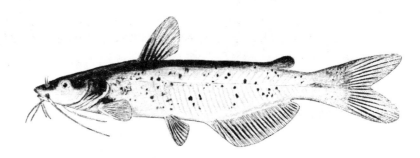

How to Catch...Catfish

Catfish are widespread and abundant in Northern California lakes and rivers. And despite their unappetizing appearance, and somewhat negative image, catfish are very good eating(catfish are not as difficult to clean as one might suspect, either). The delicious meals provided by catfish are attested to by the existence of hundreds of catfish farms, primarily in the Southeastern U.S., where these fish are raised and sold to restaurants and foodstores.

Fishing Techniques

Catfishing means still fishing. And catfishing means warm weather fishing since these critters like warm water and are most active when lakes, ponds and rivers warm up in the late spring, summer and early fall. Boats are not needed for catfishing. Simply find a spot on shore where you have enough room to cast out your weighted rig. Let it sink to the bottom. Snug up the line. And wait for the prowling whiskerfish to find your offering. A bank, a dock or a pier, where you can sit on a comfortable chair, rounds out the scene.

The best catfishing and the largest catfish(they can go up to 5, 10 or 20 pounds or more) are caught after dark. From dark to midnight and the several hours before sun-up are particularly good. But many catfish, including big ones, are caught on lazy summer afternoons.

Bring several baits along. If one doesn't produce, try something else. Often, this single maneuver can make all the difference.

Tackle and Equipment

Any rod and reel combination that can cast out a rig with a ½oz. to 6 oz. sinker will do just fine. These include specialized bass fishing tackle, light to medium spinning equipment and surf casting equipment. You'll probably be better off with a longer rod(say 7-8 ft.) so longer casts are possible.

Use monofilament line, at least 10 pound test. But heavier line is no problem, say 15 to 20 pound test.

Bait and Rigging

Catfish will eat almost anything. And they feed by both sight and by smell. Their smell sensors are on their whiskers. In fact, catfish bait is often referred to as stink bait, because at times, it seems that catfish prefer smelly offerings such as beef liver, coagulated blood, chicken entrails, etc.

But in Northern California, some of the most successful bait are less repulsive. These include;

. Fresh clams(keep them on ice, pry them open with a knife, thread hook through hard outer edge).

. Night crawlers

. Anchovies

. Redworms

. Sardine chunks

. Crayfish tails

. Chicken livers

Here's the rig to use;

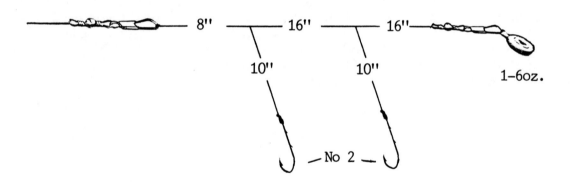

Where to Fish

Some of the best spots are in the lakes and reservoirs included in this book. The Delta and Sacramento Valley rivers are also very good. See the Lakes Section, Delta Section and Valley Rivers Section of this book.

Cleaning and Cooking

To skin a catfish, cut through the skin all around the fish, just below the gill cover. Then, using a pliers, pull the skin down the fish, while holding the fishes gills. For larger fish, it is suggested that the fish be nailed (through the head) to a tree trunk or fence post, using an adequate sized spike. The skinned catfish can then be filleted or steaked. See Fish Cleaning Section.

Catfish meat is flaky, mild with a moist texture. It is good sauteed, fried, or poached.

How to Catch...Crayfish

Why fish for crayfish, or crawdads, or crawfish anyway? Quite simply, because they're delicious - like mini-lobster! And besides, they're easy to catch and a snap to prepare. California crayfish can reach about 6 inches long and vary in color from brownish, to redish, or green-ish. Although there is no minimum size limit, most anglers return smaller crayfish(say less than 2-3 inches), since the amount of edible meat on these is slight.

Fishing Techniques

The easiest way to catch a batch of crayfish is to use one or more wire traps. These traps have funnel-shaped openings that allow the crayfish to get in, but not out. Crayfish traps are available in many bait and tackle shops. They go for about $15.00 to $20.00, but can be purchased on sale for as little as $10.00.

These traps are baited with a piece of chicken, or liver, or a can of dog food(fish flavored is good).

Perforate the dog food can with a can opener. Secure the can or other bait in the middle of the trap with a line or string. All you do is lower down the trap to the bottom on a rope and wait. Crayfish are most active at night and prefer rocky areas(that provide a place to hide). Under-cut river banks, in shady areas are also good. If evening or night fishing is not convenient, do try it in the daytime. I've seen many crayfish caught when the sun is up.

Another technique, popular with kids, is to lower a strip of bacon or piece of liver into the water using a string or fishing line. Lower it to the bottom and wait a while. Once in a while, slowly raise up the bait and ease a landing net under it, right near the surface. Usually the crayfish will hang on to the bait long enough to be caught in the net. A boat dock or tied-up houseboat is a great place to "catch crawdads" using this technique.

Caught crawfish can be stored alive for up to a day in a bucket, covered with a damp towel or gunnysack. This is important because crayfish are cooked alive(like lobster!), at least they are live when cooking starts.

Tackle and Equipment

You'll need;

. A bucket(to keep your catch in).

. A crawfish trap or two, or ...

. A pole and line(or rod, reel and line).

. Bait(dog food, chicken leg, bacon, liver).

Where to Fish

The Delta is very good. Many lakes, ponds, and streams are also good.

Cleaning and Cooking

Crayfish don't need to be cleaned. Most people cook them whole(the edible meat is in the tail and pinchers). But, some people just remove the tails and cook them. If you do this you can remove the tail by twisting and pulling it off, where it meets the body. Then grasp the middle of the three flippers at the end of the tail. Twisting and pulling it will pull out the black entrail string that runs along the top of the meat under the tail side. If it doesn't come out, don't worry. You can easily remove it after cooking, when the shell is removed.

The first step in most crayfish recipes is cooking for about 10 minutes in boiling salt water. The shell is bright red when crayfish are done. A whole crayfish can then be eaten like small lobster. Or you can clean out the meat(use a nut cracker and nut pick) and use in your favorite Newburg sauce or saute it.

CALIFORNIA HALIBUT

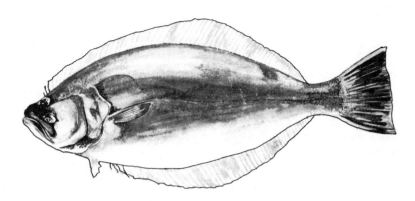

How to Catch...Halibut

Growing up in the Midwest, as we did, halibut was one of the few store-bought fish that our family enjoyed. As a boy, I didn't know where halibut came from(except from the ocean), what they looked like(I had no idea halibut had both eyes on the same side of their head), or how to catch them. But, the firm, flaky, white meat was sure a treat on our table. Everybody in Northern California is lucky to live so close to some fine halibut fishing grounds.

California halibut is a flatfish and can range in size up to 50-75 pounds. The typical keeper is from 10-20 pounds. Adult halibut move into shallower water in the late spring and summer to spawn.Young fish swim upright, but during their first year, one eye migrates to the other side of the head and they begin to swim in a horizontal position. Also, the side with the two eyes(the top) turns dark, or sand-colored, while the bottom-side turns light.

Halibut live right on the sandy bottom. A ruffling of fins and tail kicks up a cloud of sand, that settles back on the fish, hiding it from both its predators and its prey. Only its two eyes are noticeable above the sand.

Fishing Techniques

California halibut fishing is primarily shallow water fishing. Because of this situation, it is possible to catch halibut from piers, by surf casting on beaches, or from a boat. In all these cases, the basic idea is the same, get your offering down on the sandy bottom and keep it moving.

Pier anglers should cast out, let their offering sink to the bottom, and then retrieve. Move along the pier, putting special attention on casts just at the surf line.

Surf anglers have much more latitude. They can move along the beach, but can't reach as far out as pier casters.

Pier fishing techniques are described in detail starting on page 124. For surf fishing details see the section beginning on page 118. And drift fishing from a boat is covered in its own section starting on page 121.

Fishing for halibut from a boat can be done by casting or drift fishing but trolling is often preferred to cover a wider territory. Troll slowly. Halibut do school, so if one is located, chances are there are more in the same location.

Halibut feed most actively during moving current, especially on an incoming tide. The 2 to 3 hours before a high tide are often the best. And even slack water at high tide can be productive.

Fishing at the right time of year is critical to success. Summertime is when the halibut are in the shallow water. June is not too early in some locations, and July and August are usually good. Weekly fishing reports in newspapers highlight the best time.

Tackle and Equipment

Basically, anglers can fish with any rod and reel equipment that is capable of;

    1) Casting a reasonable distance.

    2) Landing a 20-30 pound game fish.

If you're a dedicated troller, you can use an ocean trolling rod and reel or ocean bottom fishing equipment. If you have surf casting equipment, you can use it on the beach or pier. If you have a medium weight spinning rod and reel(say for striper fishing or salmon fishing), that's fine.

On any equipment, use 20 pound test line, or heavier. Some halibut anglers use a 60 pound, or so, leader, because halibut have sharp teeth. You should also have a fish billy. A sharp blow midway down the body is recommended.

Boat fishermen need a large landing net. Pier anglers should have a crab ring net to raise up the fish.

Lures and Bait

Common bait and lures used for halibut are;

- Anchovies, shiners, small perch - live, hooked through lips for drifting. Hooked on a salmon rig when trolling.

- Hair Raisers ⎤
- Pet Spoons ⎬—— 1/2 - 3/4 oz.
- Kastmasters ⎦

- Rebel minnow-type plug - about 6-7 inches.

- Bagley Bango-B deep diving plug - 6-9 inches (blue back, silver belly, bleeding gills) model has been "hot" in San Francisco Bay.

When trolling a deep diving lure like the Bango-B, attach it to a snap swivel and troll it out about 50 feet behind the boat. Adjust boat speed so lure touches the bottom now and then.

Trolling rig is shown below;

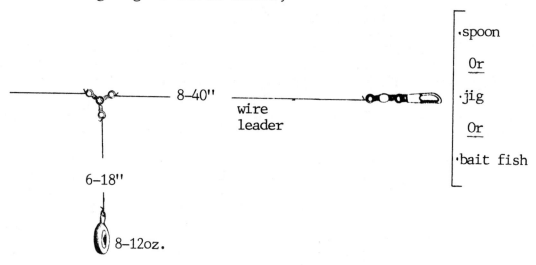

Where to Fish

Some of the best spots for halibut fishing in San Francisco Bay are detailed on page 206. In open ocean bays like Monterey Bay, troll off sandy beaches in 8-10 feet of water just outside the surf line.

Cleaning and Cooking

Smaller halibut can be filleted. Larger ones are steaked. If you can get a decent-sized steak out of your halibut, then steak it. Even when filleting, the tail section can be steaked. When filleting, first make a vertical cut(the fish is laying flat) along the lateral line down to the spine. This allows you to "lift off" two manageable-sized fillet from each side of the fish.

Halibut is dense, mild, somewhat sweet and low in fat. Popular cooking methods include broiling, barbecuing, poaching, frying, baking. The fillets can be sauteed.

KOKANEE SALMON

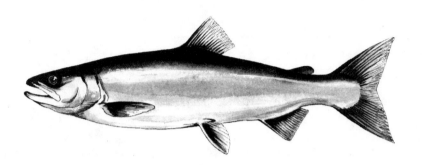

How to Catch...Kokanee

Kokanee are a land-locked sockeye salmon. They were originally planted in western reservoirs in the late 1940's. Today, the kokanee fisheries are quite active in selected Northern California locations. Specific information on the best lakes for kokanee fishing is detailed in the lake secion of the book.

Kokanee reach adulthood in about 4 years, the same as for other slamon. They spawn in late summer or fall, in lake tributaries. Kokanee can reach a length of 16 to 20 inches or more, but the overcrowding of the species(and resulting need to share a limited food resource), generally results in mature kokanee in the 8 to 14 inch range. Even at this modest size, they are a desirable catch because they taste great.

Plankton is the main food source of kokanee, so fishing for them requires an offering that provides color and movement to get their attention. They are a school fish, so once one is located, the chances of catching more, are good.

Fishing Techniques

The almost universal technique for catching kokanee is trolling. Like other salmon, kokanee prefer cold water. About 50°, in fact. This means that when a lake is stratified the kokanee are down deep. However, in spring and late fall, kokanee can be trolled for near the surface.

The approaches used for kokanee trolling have much in common with lake trolling for trout. In fact, identical equipment and rigging is used. Lake trolling for trout is described in detail in the section Trout(Lakes). Rather than repeat all this information here, let's just highlight the few differences and the key points to success;

- The most popular lures are nickel/red head, fire/pearl, rainbow and pearl/red head. Small spoons are most popular; Needlefish and Superduper, Size #1.

- In very cold clear water, it is possible to troll near the surface using this type of rig;

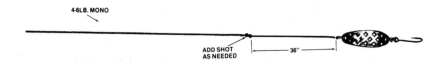

4-6LB. MONO

ADD SHOT
AS NEEDED

36"

- However, when kokanee are down more than 10 feet(the usual situation) the rig on the next page is typical;

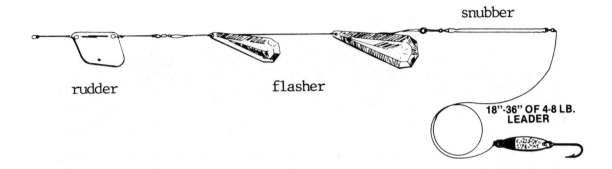

snubber

rudder

flasher

18"-36" OF 4-8 LB.
LEADER

. A rubber snubber is necessary because kokanee
  have soft, delicate mouths. The snubber absorbs
  the shock of the strike.

. A diving plane or lead core line can be trolled
  down to about 40 feet. Downriggers are better
  suited below 40 feet.

. Use the same trolling techniques as used for
  trout;

    - troll slow
    - work in S pattern
    - vary speed often

. A depth sounder can locate the school of kokanee and tell you what depth to troll.

. Many kokanee anglers add a single kernel of
  white corn, a small pinch of worm, a salmon egg,
  or a short piece of red or white yarn to the hook
  of their lure. Try it if action is slow.

Cleaning and Cooking

Most anglers clean and prepare kokanee the same as
they would small trout — See Trout(stream) Section. Kokanee have a very mild salmon-type meat.

How to Catch... Lingcod

Guess what? Lingcod aren't any closer to being a cod, than rock cod are. But, at least, unlike rock cod, lingcod don't come in every color of the rainbow. Lingcod are actually a greenling, and are rockfish. But they're much larger and tougher than other rockfish. Lings can reach upwards of 5 feet and weigh up to 70 pounds.

Fishing Techniques

Lingcod can be caught at any time of the year. And many are caught by rock cod fishermen, particularly while fishing in deep water (200-400 feet). In fact, at times a large ling will strike a small rock cod that has just been hooked.

Dedicated lingcod pursuers, however, choose to fish in fall and winter. Three of the best months are December, January and February. During this period, lings are more active, and move into shallower water to spawn.

Lingcod fishing, like rock cod fishing, is bottom, drift fishing. It is done over rocks, or reefs. Once the rig has been lowered to the bottom, it should be jigged up and down. Try to stay just off the bottom to prevent snags.

Tackle and Equipment

You'll need a gaff(lings will tear up a landing net), a fish billie(to subdue this fish that has sharp teeth and fins) and a needlenose pliers(to take out the hook).

The tackle you'll need is the same as needed for deep water rock fishing;

. Medium heavy to heavy roller-tipped, 6-7 ft. rod.

. A 6/0 or 4/0 ocean reel.

. 30-50 pound monofilament line.

Lures and Bait

The most commonly used lure for lingcod is the chrome hex bar with treble hook. The appropriate lures range from 6 to 15 ounces, depending on ocean conditions, and lings preference. Some fishermen remove the strong treble hook that comes on this lure and replace it with light wire treble hooks. The light hook bends and gives when hung-up in the rocks, before the line breaks, thus saving the expensive(about $5.00) hex bar.

Many lingcod fishermen prefer bait fishing. The best bait is whole fish. Good choices include sandabs, rock cod or squid(some anglers cut the dorsal fin off rock cod used as bait. They say it makes the bait more appetizing). It's best if the bait is alive, or at least freshly caught. 7-10 inches is a good size.

Use a two hook rig. The end hook goes through the

bait fishes upper lip(or through both lips) and the other hook goes into the side of the fish near the tail.

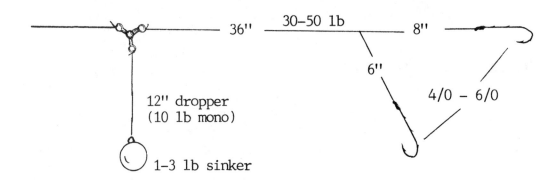

Where to Fish

See Ocean Fishing Section of this book.

Cleaning and Cooking

Lingcod are most often filleted. Larger ones can be steaked.

Lingcod fillets or steaks are lean and mild tasting. Lingcod meat(depending on the age of the fish and where it is caught) is often green, but turns white upon cooking. Thick fillets or steaks can be barbecued or broiled. They are also suitable for poaching or frying. Thinner fillets can be sauteed. Lingcod is rather dense, so it takes somewhat longer to cook.

BLACK CRAPPIE

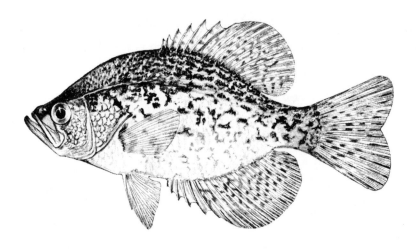

How to Catch...Panfish

Bluegills, crappies, perch and other varieties of panfish are plentiful in many Northern California lakes, as well as in the Delta. These fish are fun to catch and are very enjoyable eating. And in many locations, they are abundant, so there is no need to feel guilty about taking them. They reproduce with great success and heavy populations can crowd out larger sportfish.

Panfishing is easy and relaxing fishing. And it is especially enjoyable for youngsters.

Still Fishing

Still fishing is probably the most popular approach. It can be done from shore or from an anchored or drifting boat(once fish are located, a drifting boat should be anchored). Still fishing for panfish can be done with just about any light tackle, including spinning equipment(probably the most common), spincasting equipment, baitcasting equipment, a flyrod and reel, or a cane pole.

From boat, shore or dock you can use a bobber rig;

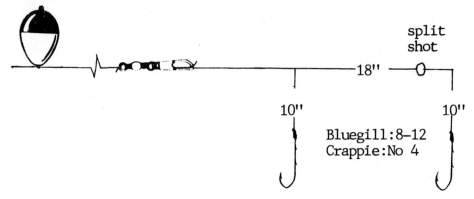

From a boat or dock you can use the same bobber rig or take it off and fish straight below the pole or rod tip.

If the fish are feeding near the bottom, a sliding sinker rig works good from shore or boat. This set up has an advantage in that it stays put, whereas a bobber rig drifts with the breeze. Of course, a bobber rig is less likely to get caught on the bottom, and is good when fish are near the surface or suspended;

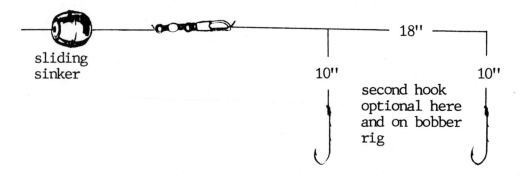

Still fishing for panfish might be somewhat of a misnomer. Most experts agree that a slight movement of your bait is desirable. With any rig, flick the rod tip frequently to move your bait. Another basic principle is to change depths, if action is slow. Frequently, larger panfish are down deeper than most bobber anglers suspect.

Many baits are successful. Redworms, minnows, crickets, grasshoppers, commercial dough-type bait are all good. Check with your local bait supplier for the latest information.

Jigging

Jigging for panfish is best done from a boat, or from a pier or dock. It involves lowering a crappie or mini-jig to right near the bottom. Here again, movement is important. Twitch the rod tip and lift it slightly every once in a while. Jigging can be done with just about any lightweight fishing tackle. There are many mini-jigs available, but white or yellow are very popular. They can be purchased just about everywhere at a very reasonable price.

Fly Fishing

Flycasting for panfish is enjoyable and productive. A medium action, 7½-8½ rod is suggested, but any will do. A wide variety of offerings will produce depending on the lake, the time of year and the time of day;

- Panfish poppers - swim them slowly along in a stop and go fashion.

- Dry flys, size 10 or 12.

- Wet flys, size 10 or 12.

- Bucktail streamers, size 8.

- Nymphs(black and white, white, brown, etc.).

- Indiana spinners(2 blades, #8).

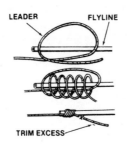

Bobber Casting

A casting bobber is a small bobber, usually made of clear plastic that is attached to monofilament line. Because of its weight(some allow you to let in water to make it even heavier) it allows anglers to cast poppers, flys, etc., using spinning, spincasting or baitcasting equipment. So you can enjoy "fly fishing" without having to use a flyrod and reel.

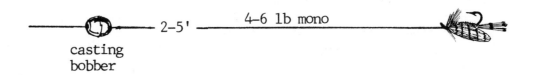

casting
bobber

Where to Fish

Like many fish, panfish can often be found in shallower water(5-10 feet) in spring and in deeper water in summer (10-30 feet). Like bass, panfish like to be near something (like a drop off, a brush pile, a weed bed, or the bottom), although, at times, they will suspend in deeper water. It's generally true that the larger fish are down deeper. Whenever you find smaller fish along a point or bar, follow it out, looking for a steeper dropoff. This is where bigger fish might be found. In summer, check submerged creek channels and areas directly out from where you found them in the spring. Rowing several baited, or jig-rigged poles, with offerings at varying depths, will often locate a school of nice fish.

See Lake and Delta Maps for specifics on panfish locations.

Cleaning and Cooking

Most people clean panfish in the traditional way. Scale them by rubbing a knife or scaling tool from the tail of the fish to the head. Cut open the belly and remove the guts. Finally, cut off the head. Rinse them off and they're ready for the pan.

An alternative is to fillet them. This yields a little less meat, but eliminates skin and bone in the cooked fish. See instructions on filleting, in the Fish Cleaning section of this book.

Sauteeing the whole fish or individual fillets is most popular. Pieces cut off fillets can be battered and deep fried, and are delicious.

CABEZON

How to Catch... **Rock Cod**

Rock cod are not actually cod, but a group of ocean dwelling bottom fish. They are fun to catch and delicious to eat. Varieties of rock cod include fish with names such as blues, reds, yellowtail, cabezon and browns. Rockfish run up to 7-10 pounds, but average 2-4 pounds. These fish are quite ugly, with large mouths and sharp pointed fins, but they produce delicious fillets.

Fishing Techniques

Rockfishing for most anglers means drift fishing from a boat. It can be done as close in as ½ mile from shore to as far out as the Farallon Islands, or other offshore reef areas.

The technique is quite simple. With the use of a depth sounder, locate the boat over a rocky bottom. Often the best location is one where a depth is changing, either on the upslope of a canyon or on the changing slope of a reef.

Now just lower your rig over the side until you feel the weight hit the bottom. Put the reel into gear, and crank up a foot or two. Check for the bottom, by lowering your line frequently, to avoid drifting into snags, or letting your bait move too far from the bottom. Jigging (moving your offering up and down a few feet) is also a good idea. The motion catches the eye of the rockfish.

Sometimes rockfish are also caught alongside kelp beds in the shallows near shore. Again, fish near the bottom and reel in fast to keep the fish from snagging in the kelp.

Tackle and Equipment

The heft or weight of the tackle needed for rockfishing depends primarily on the depth of water you're fishing in;

	50-100 Feet	300-400 Feet
Rod:		
-length	6 to 7 ft.	6 to 7 ft.
-stiffness	Med-Med. Heavy	Med. Heavy - Heavy
-guide	roller tip helpful	roller
Reel:	Medium ocean bait-casting	Penn Senator 114 6/0
Line:	25-40 lb. mono	40-80 lb. mono
Sinker:	4 oz.- 1 lb.	½ - 2 lb.

At the end of your line, fasten a heavy swivel snap. To this, attach a rock cod rig or shrimp fly rig with 6/0 size hooks. I prefer the shrimp fly rig since they have feathers that add to the attractiveness of the offering. Shrimp fly rigs can be purchased in most ocean fishing-oriented bait and tackle shops for less than a dollar each. They typically have 3 hooks and a snap swivel at the end to attach the sinker.

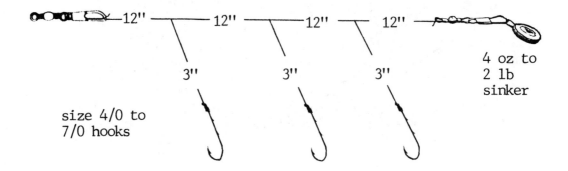

—12" — — 12" — — 12" — — 12" —

3"   3"   3"

4 oz to
2 lb
sinker

size 4/0 to
7/0 hooks

Bait and Rigging

The most common bait for rockfishing is cut-up squid
pieces. Cut the pieces large enough to cover the hook.
Other common baits are pieces of small rock fish and anchovies. At times fish can be hooked using bare shrimp fly
rigs. But, bait adds an odor that is often helpful in
enticing a bite.

Where to Fish

See Ocean Fishing maps.

Cleaning and Cooking

Rockfish are almost always filleted. Since almost all
varieties of rockfish(or rock cod) have very large heads,
the yield of fillets can be as low as 20-30% of fish weight.
Rock cod meat is lean, has low fat content and is mild tasting. These fillets lend themselves to the cooking method
of choice including sauteeing, broiling, poaching, frying
or baking.

How to Catch...Rock Crab

Anglers who fish in the shallow Pacific waters near breakwaters and wharfs are often frustrated by rock crabs steeling their bait. Rather than getting mad at these plentiful pirates, why not get even...by catching them and eating them? These relatives of the Dunganess crab have large pincers that are just as tasty.

Fishing Techniques

Rock crab fishing is simple and leisurely. All you need is a hoop net and about 75 to 100 feet of rope(nylon or clothesline will do). Rock crab nets are sold in many fishing tackle shops for less that $20. Ask the shop how to attach the rope to the particular net you purchase.

The most common bait is a fish carcass...or what's left after a large rockfish has had its fillets removed. They come either fresh or fresh frozen, at bait shops (especially those on or near popular public wharfs).

One rule of thumb holds true; the more bait in the net, the more rock crabs you'll catch. Crabs find the bait by smelling it. So more bait gets more smell into the water.

The fish carcasses are tied to the bottom of the net. Once out on a jetty or wharf, simply lower the baited net into the water, all the way to the bottom. With a little experience you'll realize how often the net should be raised up to the water surface for checking. When a rock crab is spotted in the net, quickly raise it up all the way. Remove it from the net(but avoid the pincers) and place it in a bucket of sea water. Lower the net and haul up some more.

Timing will improve your catch. Crabbing is often best just before and after the peak of high tide. A three hour period centered around high tide is recommended.

Bait and Rigging

. A hoop net.

. 100 feet of rope or line(strong enough to lower and raise the net).

. A large bucket.

. Fresh fish carcasses.

Where to Fish

Piers, wharfs and rocky breakwaters or jettys along the Pacific coastline are most popular.

Cleaning and Cooking

Rock crabs are cooked and eaten like lobster. Most of the meat is in the pincers. Cook crabs in boiling water until shells turn red(about 10 minutes).

KING SALMON

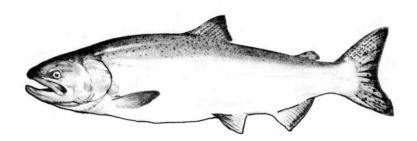

How to Catch...Salmon(in the Ocean)

Both king(chinook) and silver(coho) salmon are caught in Northern California ocean waters. But kings are by far the most common. The salmon in California salt water were spawned naturally, or in hatcheries, in tributaries of coastal rivers like the Klamath, Trinity, and Sacramento. About 60% of California ocean caught salmon originate in the Sacramento River system(including the Feather and American Rivers).

The limit for salmon is 2, with a minimum length of 20 inches. Only one single, barbless hook(either manufactured that way, or with the barb flattened using a pliers) is allowed per rod.

Undersize fish(called shakers) should be released without netting or handling. A needle-nosed pliers is needed. This prevents the fragile, protective membrane on the body of the fish from being broken. Grasp the leader about 2 feet up from the hook. Next grasp the hook shank with the pliers(or slide a rod or stiff wire into the curve of the hook). Now, raise and rotate the hook upside down. The salmon will drop off into the ocean.

It's obviously easier for a salmon to throw a barbless hook, so slack line condition must be avoided when playing a fish. Once a keeper salmon is netted, it should be clubbed between the eyes, with a hammer handle or fish club, to subdue it. Most seasoned fishermen gill and gut salmon when caught, and then store them in an iced fish box or cooler. The tail is clipped to distinguish from commercially caught salmon.

Fishing Techniques

There are four primary techniques for taking salmon in saltwater;

1. Trolling with a diving plane.

2. Trolling with a cannonball sinker with sinker release.

3. Trolling with a downrigger.

4. Mooching - Basically drift fishing with bait. This method is growing in popularity, but trolling still probably yields 95% or more of the sport angling salmon catch.

Trolling

The most common method for taking ocean salmon in California waters is trolling, or pulling a lure or bait through the water using boat movement. Since king salmon especially, are often found 10 to 100 feet below the surface, methods must be employed to take bait or lures to these depths. That's where diving planes, cannonballs with sinker releases and downriggers come in.

Diving Plane - a weighted, air foil device that uses the motion of the water to dive and takes the terminal tackle with it. After a salmon strike, the diving plane neutralizes its position, allowing the rig and fish to rise up to the surface.

Cannonball-Sinker Release - This approach relies on the heft of a steel or lead cannonball of 1, 2, or 3 pounds to take the rigging down. The cannonballs are attached to a sinker release mechanism which releases the weight when a salmon hits, allowing the fish to rise and fight.

Downrigger - A pully and boom assembly(manually or electrically activated) which lowers a 10 pound weight on a steel cable. A clip holds the rod's fishing line and releases it when a salmon strikes.

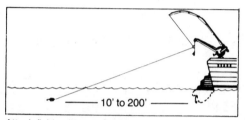

Attach fishing line to weight.

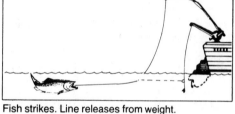

Fish strikes. Line releases from weight.

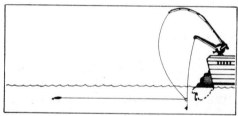

Lower to desired fishing depth.

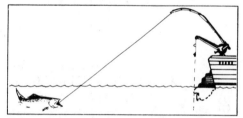

Fight and land fish (weight returned to boom tip).

Trolling with a diving plane or cannonball-sinker release works like this. With the boat at trolling speed (2-4 knots) lower the terminal tackle in the water, check lure action, then let out about 24-40 pulls of line(this puts the hook at about 15-20 feet deep). Other rods should be deeper or shallower until fish are located. Put on clicker and then set drag just tight enough to hold the line. Put the rod in a holder. The singing drag will signal a strike. The pull of the salmon will drop the weight or open the diving plane, allowing the fish to rise and fight. Some anglers maintain trolling speed while fighting the fish. This minimizes the chance of slack line and a thrown hook. The landing net should always be placed from the front, forward and under the fish.

Trolling with a downrigger has several advantages. It allows deep trolling(50-100 feet) without the use of heavy rods/reels and line. And the downrigger "tells you" exactly how deep you're trolling, so successes can be duplicated. Downriggers cost between $100.00-300.00 and probably are not necessary, or some say, desirable if the fish are at 10 to 40 feet. Beyond 40 feet they are very useful. Downriggers are also very useful for trolling for trout and salmon in lakes during the summertime when these fish are 50-100 feet down.

Mooching

Mooching, or drift fishing, for salmon can be very effective and quite exciting if you can locate the fish. Feeding birds are one clue. Fish locators are also helpful to select the proper depth to fish. Often, mooching is done just off the bottom, with a whole anchovie rigged on a 3/0 or 4/0 hook.

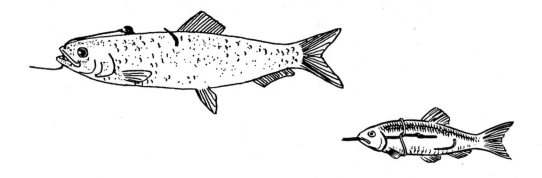

Use only enough weight to hold the bait down at a 50-60° angle. Dangle the offering. Lift the rod tip, come up a few cranks, wait. Lower it and repeat the process. Often the salmon will "bump" the bait a few times before striking solidly. Don't set the hook until a substantial strike is felt.

Tackle and Equipment

No matter which approach you use you should have;

. Large cooler with ice

. Fish club or hammer

. Needle-nose pliers

. Large landing net

For trolling with a diving plane or weight you'll need;

. Medium heavy or heavy boat rod with roller tip, about 6 feet.

. Salt water trolling or casting reel that can hold 300 yards of 25 lb. test monofilament line. Spinning reels or levelwind reels are not generally used.

The terminal tackle with diving plane includes a dodger to attract salmon;

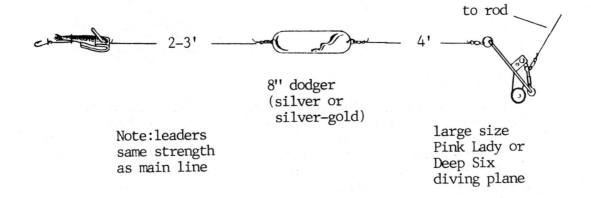

2-3'

8" dodger
(silver or
silver-gold)

Note: leaders
same strength
as main line

to rod

4'

large size
Pink Lady or
Deep Six
diving plane

Terminal tackle with cannonball-sinker release is illustrated on next page;

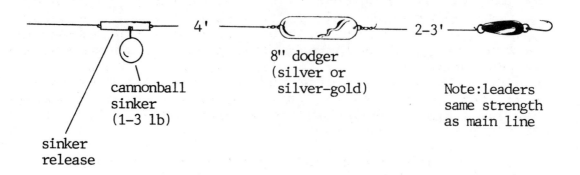

cannonball
sinker
(1-3 lb)

sinker
release

8" dodger
(silver or
silver-gold)

Note:leaders
same strength
as main line

For trolling with a downrigger you'll need;

. The downrigger

. Bait casting or spinning rod of 6-8 feet

. Bait casting or spinning reel that can hold
  200 yards of 10-20 lb. monofilament line

For mooching you'll need the same types of rod/reel
combinations used for downrigging.

Lures and Bait

The most popular bait for ocean salmon is anchovies.
They are purchased frozen, laying flat on a plastic tray,
from bait shops. For trolling, the anchovie is either
rigged on a crowbar hook or on a plastic bait holding rig.

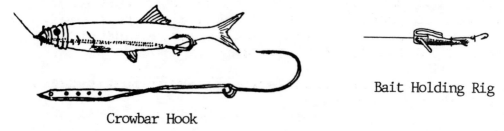

Crowbar Hook

Bait Holding Rig

It's crucial that the anchovies, when trolled, roll or wobble, like a wounded bait fish. Without practice or specific experience, this is difficult, using the crowbar hook. But, with the plastic bait holding rig(common brand names; Rotary Salmon Killer, Herring Aid), a rolling action is guaranteed because of the fin-shape molded into the plastic. Also, putting the anchovie into either of these rigs takes only a few seconds. Commercial salmon fishermen typically rig crowbar hooks in advance, because it requires patience and a steady hand.

Some Silver Spoons and lures that imitate squid (commonly called hoochies) can also be effective;

. Krocidile - 1 and 2 oz.

. Hopkins Spoon - 3/4 oz.

. McMahon Spoon - No. 4(half brass-half silver).

. Hoochie(hula skirt jig) - about 3-4 inches, assorted colors.

Where to Fish

See Ocean and San Francisco Bay fishing maps.

Cleaning and Cooking

Salmon are usually filleted. Larger ones are steaked.

Fresh salmon and properly frozen fresh salmon, as anyone knows who has eaten it, is out of this world. Many anglers prefer to barbecue this rich, relatively fat meat. It is also very good poached(served hot with a sauce, or chilled), broiled, baked or smoked.

Scale salmon with the jet of a water hose nozzle.

AMERICAN SHAD

How to Catch...Shad

Veteran shad anglers consider this fish the best
fighter, pound-for-pound, of available fish in Northern
California waters. Shad spawn in the Sacramento River
and its tributaries(American, Feather, Yuba) in late
spring and early summer. Fishermen usually begin their
shad quest in late April or early May. A typical American shad weighs-in at 3 to 5 pounds.

Fishing Techniques

Casting is the predominant technique for taking shad.
Shad strike very aggressively at small, silver objects
that show bright colors such as red, orange, green, white
and yellow. But, most of these strikes don't result in
hook-ups. Shad are more protective of their territory,
than hungry, at this time of year, so they are difficult
to hook. They fight savagely, so a hook-up doesn't necessarily result in a fish in hand.

Casting is done both from shore and from anchored boats, depending on local river conditions. Shore fishing is done mostly where there is a shoal in the bend of a river. Deeper water and the availability of launch ramp facilities provides the opportunity for boat fishing.

One shad fishing technique which is commonly used, particularly at the mouth of the American River, involves fishing from an anchored boat in a relatively strong current, using a spinning or baitcasting rod. A small lead sinker is placed at the end of the line, and a weighted fly is tied on a 24 inch dropper about 18 inches above the sinker. The line is played out until the sinker just clears the bottom. It is necessary for the current to be strong enough to give the fly the proper action. This method of fishing has so many followers that space to anchor at the mouth of the American River is often at a premium. Shore anglers at the mouth of the American River successfully use spinning gear and a floating plastic bubble attached about three feet above the offering.

You can buy many types of shad lures and flies in Sacramento Valley sporting goods stores and on a weekend during a good run, even shore anglers may find it difficult to locate a place to fish. Nevertheless, the most popular method of shad angling in California, and perhaps the most rewarding, is to fish from shore with a fly rod or a spinning rod. The fly rod is used with a fast-sinking line or a shooting head. A tippet with about a 6 pound test breaking strength is desirable since the shad can be quite large. Some will exceed 5 or 6 pounds. In addition, there is always the possibility of hooking a striped bass or a large steelhead.

Let us assume you have found a likely spot on a river, just below a riffle where the fast water breaks and slows down at the head of a long pool. You wade out into the water and cast across toward the opposite bank, allowing the current to swing your line downstream. You wait a few moments as the fly at the end of your tautening line makes its way downstream and toward the bank below you. As you are ready to pick up and cast again, you hook your first shad and are in for a delightful surprise. Before long, on a typical day, you may repeat this experience again and again until you have caught and released or kept, a considerable number of fish.

If you use a spinning outfit, the shad fly is tied to the end of the line and a split shot is pinched on from 18 to 24 inches above the fly. Just enough weight is used to enable you to cast easily. Cast out across the water as you would with a fly rod, but immediately after completing your cast, reel in just fast enough to prevent the split shot from snagging the bottom.

Tackle and Equipment

Shad fishing means light tackle fishing. Equipment must be light enough and flexible enough to toss small offerings. Anyway, the light tackle makes for more challenge. Spinning, fly fishing and baitcasting set-ups are all used. Popular lures include Katydids, Mr. Twister, Mini-jigs, and Flea Flies.

Where to Fish

Good areas are described in the Valley River Section. Specific locations are best determined from local bait and tackle shops. Here are general guidelines;

- Yuba - from the mouth upstream to Daguerre Point Dam.

- Feather - from the mouth to fish barrier at Oroville.

- American - from the mouth to Nimbus Dam.

Cleaning and Cooking

Many anglers release shad because they are so bony. And filleting a shad is no easy task, even after you've seen it done by an expert. The Department of Fish and Game tried a number of years ago, to encourage the eating of shad. They did this by publishing a booklet that describes How To Fillet A Shad - In 32 Steps! Step 32 concludes, "In a little while, with some patience, you will be able to trim a shad into two boneless fillets in about 15 to 20 minutes."

Shad is mild, quite firm, with a meatlike flavor and a moderate fat level. It is good baked, poached or smoked.

BLUE SHARK

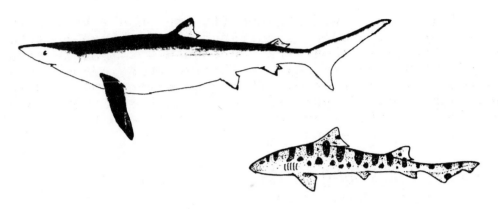

LEOPARD SHARK

How to Catch...Sharks

Shark are a misrepresented fish. All the media ever talk about are great white sharks. But there are other varieties of shark in Northern California waters. These include leopard shark, sevengill and sixgill cow shark and blue shark. What's more, the media never mentions that these sharks are becoming more and more popular among sports fishing people; popular to fish for and popular to eat.

Sevengill and sixgill cow sharks can get quite large. The largest sevengill shark caught was over 500 pounds. It's quite possible to hook fish in the 200 pound range. However, the most common shark caught in Northern California waters is the leopard shark. These can weigh up to about 30 pounds and are about 4 feet in length. The average fish is between 10 and 20 pounds.

Fishing Techniques

Most shark fishing is done from an anchored boat,

using a sliding sinker rig and fishing on the bottom.
It's the same approach used when still fishing for striped
bass. The rig is baited up and tossed out. Depressions
in the bottom or deep holes are prime spots. An incoming tide, just past slack, is a good time to fish. Always keep an eye on your rod tip(or hold your rod). When
the tip moves, point the rod at the fish and then set the
hook hard on the second tug.

Sharks should always be landed with a gaff. I made
the mistake of landing a relatively small leopard shark,
that my son had hooked, in my salmon landing net. The
shark actually bit its way out. A fish club is also needed to dispense sharks.

Tackle and Equipment

Tackle varies, depending on the size of sharks you're
after. Heavyweight shark hunters use stiff 6-7 foot rods
with roller guides, a size ought-six conventional reel and
about 500 yards of 60-pound, wire line. But these types of
hefty equipment are by no means necessary or even desirable
for you to enjoy shark fishing. Many shark anglers use
sturgeon fishing tackle, striped bass fishing tackle, rock
cod fishing tackle, or even salmon fishing tackle. Any
tackle that can handle 20 to 30 pound test monofilament
line and an 8 ounce sinker will do for most shark fishing. The two essentials, however, are wire leaders and
a fish club.

Bait and Rigging

Several types of baits are used for shark. These
include anchovies, squid, salmon bellies, and a bullhead-
type baitfish known as "lordfish" or "midshipman". Non-
conventional baits include chicken parts, calves liver, etc.
Within this wide array, the best are probably whole squid,
pieces of salmon belly and lordfish. Squid are most read-
ily available, but attract nuisance fish(small rays, too
small sharks and crabs).

The hook should be run through the squid several times, and check your bait frequently. Pieces of salmon belly are difficult to come by, but work well. Lordfish are caught as a by-product of shrimping. They work well because smaller nuisance fish don't seem interested in them. Conventional party boat captains often use midshipman as bait. Typical shark rig is below;

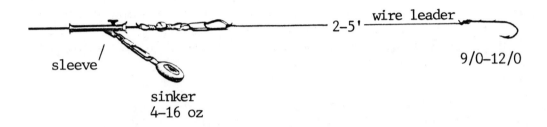

sleeve

sinker
4-16 oz

2-5' ——— wire leader

9/0-12/0

Where to Fish

Most shark fishing is done in bay waters.

Good spots for leopard shark include;

. The area off Pt. Richmond

. Hunter's Point off San Francisco

. The channel near Dumbarton Bridge in South San Francisco Bay

Good spots for large six and seven gill sharks include;

. "Big Hole" - just west of Angel Island

- "The Greenhouse" - just off the Marin shore-line just south of Sausalito(look for small green building at the bottom of the cliff).

- The channel from Oakland to the San Mateo Bridge in South San Francisco Bay.

Use a depthfinder and chart of the bottom, or a chart recorder to locate deep holes or underwater shelves.

Cleaning and Cooking

Smaller sharks are easily filleted. Larger sharks are generally steaked. Final trimming should remove any red meat to eliminate any chance of a fleshy taste. Remove the tough skin because it shrinks a good deal during cooking.

Shark meat is firm, white and very low in fat and has a mild to moderate flavor. Shark is well suited to baking, poaching, barbecuing, deep-frying and as a nice addition to soup, stews and casseroles. It is also delicious smoked.

STEELHEAD RAINBOW TROUT

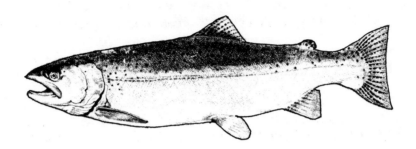

How to Catch...Steelhead and Salmon(in Rivers)

Steelhead and salmon fishing in coastal rivers and streams and in the Sacramento River system is one of the most pleasurable and rewarding of all fishing experiences. Many veteran anglers, who have fished all over the world, insist that steelhead and salmon fishing is the ultimate fishing experience, despite the wind, rain and cold. Anglers endure and overcome wet and cold because the fall and winter months are when ocean-toughened, acrobatic steelhead trout(actually a variety of rainbow trout) and large king(chinook) salmon migrate into fresh water to spawn.

Early fall steelhead are often juvenile fish that don't spawn. These are called "half-pounders" even though they run from ½-2 pounds. Mature spawning steelhead that migrate later in fall and in winter average 5 to 10 pounds, with fish in some streams reaching up to 15-20 pounds.

The migrating king salmon(some streams also have runs of smaller silver, or coho salmon) are larger fish, on average, than those caught in the ocean during spring and summer. This is because only the mature adult fish join the spawning run. They move up river to their spawning beds, spawn and die, their life cycle complete. Steelhead, on the other hand, will spawn and return to the ocean several times. King salmon catches are in the 10-20 pound range with occassional fish going as high as 40 pounds. The record, caught on the Sacramento River near Redbluff in 1979, weighed in at 88 pounds! Fresh run salmon are bright, much like ocean-caught salmon. As spawning time comes closer, salmon turn dark, and are not good eating. These should probably be released to spawn.

Sometimes it is difficult to distinguish between king salmon, silver salmon and steelhead trout. Here are some basic keys;

King Salmon - On the lower jaw, the crown of the gums where the teeth project, is dark, as is the rest of the mouth. There are usually large, angular black spots on the back and both lobes of the tail.

Silver Salmon - The crown of the gums where the teeth project(lower jaw) is whitish, the rest of the mouth lining is darker. There are usually spots on the back and upper lobe of the tail, but none on the lower lobe.

Steelhead Trout - The inside of the mouth is whitish. There are teeth on the tip but not on the back of the tongue.

Steelhead and salmon that are migrating in fresh water are not particularly interested in eating. In fact, all agree, that salmon don't eat at all. And steelhead eat little or nothing. This situation means that anglers can't rely on a fishes appetite to induce a strike. Most experts feel that steelhead and salmon strike out of instinct, curiosity, or most likely to protect their territory. They will not move far to take an offering, most stay only a few inches to either side of their hold.

In some coastal streams, particularly the Klamath and Trinity, there are summer-run steelhead. These steelhead eat and behave and often take on the appearance of rainbow trout(because they are in fresh water 6-10 months before spawning in the spring). Summer-run steelhead are caught using Stream Trout Fishing Techniques. See Catching Trout(in streams) Section.

Some steelhead salmon anglers use boats. Others fish from shore or use waders. Boats are useful in some streams when private property limits access or where a boat can provide access to an area too steep to climb down to from a road or tract. Boat anglers can cover much more potentially good fishing spots in a day than the shore anglers can. One highly specialized and highly successful steelhead and salmon fishing technique called backtrolling, requires a boat. More on this later.

The fishing techniques, bait, lures, tackle and equipment are the same or similar for both steelhead and salmon fishing. There are several exceptions and these will be noted and explained in the sections that follow.

Fishing Techniques

All steelhead and salmon fishing techniques have one common denominator. They are designed to get a lure or bait right down on the bottom of the stream. This is the only place the fish are, and in the winter, when they're not eating, they won't move up to take an offering. A lure or bait that's not within several inches of the bottom has almost as little chance of catching a fish as those still sitting on a shelf in the tackle shop. An old saying goes like this, "If you're not losing terminal tackle you're not fishing deep enough." Unfortunately, for our pocketbooks, but fortunately, for tackle manufacturers, this statement is all too true. Happily, there are rigs and approaches that minimize the loss due to hangups, and these are emphasized here.

We know that salmon and steelhead are on the bottom of the stream or river. The next question, where along all that bottom are we most likely to find them? Here are the choice spots;

   . At a tributary stream mouth(in fact, some of these are so productive that they are closed to fishing for a certain period each year. See individual river regulations).

- Just off the main current of a river in water 3-8 feet deep. Not in the very fast water, but not in backwater either.

- At the head or tail end of a deep hole. Salmon in the Sacramento River system are pursued in holes deeper than 10 feet.

- Along a deep side channel.

- Just above or below a riffle.

- A few feet behind a slick formed by the current breaking around a boulder(this includes submerged boulders and bridge pilings and abutments that are "artificial" boulders).

- The tidal basin of the river or stream and the upper limit of high tide in any stream. Pools and holes in these sections are good.

- In small streams steelhead hold along and under sweeps of overhanging brush and foliage.

- Along underwater ledges, cliffs, or undercuts.

- In the fall, early run steelhead are frequently in riffles themselves. In small coastal streams steelhead will often hold in shallow water(a foot or so) above or within a riffle.

There are a number of approaches used to catch steelhead and salmon. Here is a rundown on each.

Drift Fishing

For those readers not familiar with coastal river fishing terminology, a brief explanation is in order. Drift fishing, in this usage, has nothing to do with a boat. Drift fishing refers to drifting a bait or lure along in the current of a river. Most anglers do this from shore or while wading out, but it sometimes is done from an anchored boat. It is actually very similar to the bait fishing approach used for trout in streams in the summertime, except the terminal tackle is heavier because the water is faster and deeper, and because the fish are larger and stronger.

The lure or bait is cast upstream at about a 45° angle and then allowed to drift down stream into likely holding areas. Slack line is taken up as the drift proceeds. A key is to use the proper weight so that the offering moves freely, yet stays on or near the bottom. A weight that is too heavy will freeze or even hang-up, while one that is too light will move off the bottom. The perfect amount of weight is that which will result in a tap-tap-skip action as is makes frequent contact with the bottom and then bounces up a bit before striking again.

Strikes are often soft in this type of fishing. The fish just mouth the offering, but don't hit it or run with it. Often, fish are lost because the angler can't differenciate between a bite and the feel of the bottom. Any momentary slowing or stopping of a drift lure or bait, should be assumed to be a take. Respond by setting the hook hard.

There are several different weight systems that drift anglers use, depending on personal preference. In all systems the weight is 18-24 inches up from the lure or bait. Leaders are the same weight as the main line. These are the popular alternatives;

   . Lead cinch - these are basically 3-way swivels, with rubber tubing attached to the middle swivel. They are available in stores. A pencil lead weight(3/16"diameter is most popular) of varying length is inserted into the tubing. It slips out to free the rig from a snag.

- Hollow pencil lead is fastened(crimped) to the knot dropper at the swivel. If hung up, it will pull away from the lead if not crimped too tight.

- 3-way swivel with dropper - use when larger weight is needed.

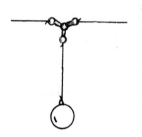

- For smaller streams a simple choice is to use a rubber core sinker. Tie the hook to the main line and put the sinker on about 18" up the line. Have a selection of sinker sizes with you.

Lures and Bait

The choice of bait and lures is very wide in drift fishing. Here are the most popular;

. Salmon roe tied in dime to quarter sized red Maline bags with thread. These are put on a special steelhead baitholding hook. Hook size #1 is good. Bags can also be put right on a regular hook.

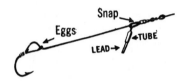

. Nightcrawlers - thread on hook. Let an inch or so at the end dangle free.

. Drift bobbers - These are not regular bobbers but boyant lures, usually bright colors and often rotate in water to send off vibrations. Some slide on the leader of the hook, after a bead to enhance rotation. Others come with metal shafts and their own treble hook. These are very productive and have replaced roe as the main offering of many anglers. Popular ones are Okie Drifters, Spin-N-Glo, and Glo-Go.

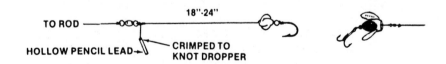

. Yarn - Yarn can be fished alone, but usually it is added to roe or drift bobber rigs. Good colors are red, orange and cerise. It enhances the offerings appearance, and gets tangled in the

fishes teeth(preventing deep hooking and
helping signal bites). Some can also be
tied to the line above the drift bobber.

. Single salmon rig - For small coastal streams,
  use a hook size that is entirely engulfed by
  the egg. Large white eggs are good. Fish with
  as little weight as possible(a few split shot
  a foot up from the hook). This system can often
  catch big fish.

Plunking

Here we have another "steelhead" word, that basically
means stillfishing. Here the anglers intentionally put
enough weight on their terminal tackle so it will not drift.
Bait or floating lures are used. The rod is then propped
up into a rod holder and coffee is poured. Actually, many
plunkers have another rod for casting to pass the idle
time. Some plunkers use a sliding sinker rig(see Catching
Trout in Lakes), while others use the same rig as drift
anglers.

Bait and lures are also the same as for drift fishing.

Casting

Casting is simply that. Weighted spinners or spoons
are cast up and across the stream and then returned. This
is an active approach but since retrieves are by necessity
near the bottom, they result in frequent hangups and loss
of lures. Of course, drift fishing also results in hangups,

but typically less costly offerings are used and rigs are used that often result in only partial loss of terminal tackle.

A small snap swivel should be used at the end of your main line to attach casting spoons and spinners. Wobbling spoons of about 1-3 inches long(e.g. Kastmaster, Daredevil) striped, dotted or solid bright flourescent hues, or in nickel, bronze or copper, are favorites. Mepps or Mounti-type spinners in nickel, brass or copper are good in size 4 and 5.

Choose the size to meet water conditions, so that the retrieve is natural and near the bottom. Heavy spoons are best in fast water. Light and narrower ones are best in quieter water. In roiled waters or at low light levels, spinners are preferred.

Backtrolling

Backtrolling is probably the most productive method of taking steelhead and salmon. It necessitates a boat. Here the anglers face the boat upstream and apply just enough power to allow the boat to slowly move downstream. A deep-diving plug, weighted plug or weighted bait is trolled off the back of the boat. Since the current is moving much faster than the boat, it takes the offering deep down in the current. The backtroller slowly works back and forth across a promising hole, then drops downstream a few feet and works across again. This approach is not recommended for anglers who are not experienced at river current boat handling.

> . Steelhead backtrollers use Hotshot(size 10,20, 30) or similar lures tied directly to the line.

. Salmon backtrollers use Flatfish, or similar, M-2, T-50 and T-55. Bags of salmon roe are tied to the treble hooks and a sardine fillet is tied to the underside of the lure.

24-30" 20 lb leader (lure)

12", 15 lb dropper

2-6 oz. sinker

Float

Drift fishing requires experience and skill, in getting the offering right on the bottom and in detecting subtle bites. Some anglers, if they're not too self-conscious, add a float or bobber to their rig to minimize these difficulties. A float set at the right distance, holds the terminal tackle off the bottom, but right near it. Take up slack line as the bobber floats downstream, and set the hook if the bobber pauses or dips.

Fly

Fly fishing equipment and techniques can be used for fall and winter run steelhead and salmon. But, it is the exception rather than the rule. Specialized knowledge and skill is needed. If you intend to pursue this area, check out some steelhead and fly fishing books from your public library.

Water

Water conditions have an effect on your lure selection and fishing technique.

Muddy Water

. Use roe, salmon eggs or nightcrawlers - anything with a scent.

. Use larger, more garish colored drift bobbers.

. Use drift bobbers that spin fast to make vibration.

Off-Colored Water

. Use drift bobbers and artificial eggs.

. Ideal steelhead and salmon water is milky-green color, dropping and clearing after a freshet.

. Fish during a new rain - fish are stimulated.

Clear Water

. Use small offering and more subdued colors.

. Spoons and spinners work good.

Tackle and Equipment

Tackle used in steelhead and salmon fishing can be quite specialized, but for most situations, basic equipment is sufficient. Here is a rundown;

. Rod - Most drift and plunker anglers use a 8-9 foot, medium action(or medium-light action) spinning or baitcasting rod, with a 2 hand grip. A sensative tip is essential. For fishing wide tidal areas from shore, some anglers use surf casting equipment. Backtrollers generally use about a 6 foot baitcasting, boat rod with medium-heavy action and a sensative tip.

- Reels - Spinning reels need to be large enough to hold 200 yards of 10 pound monofilament line and have a good drag system. Ditto for baitcasting reels. Baitcasting reels are typically levelwinds with free spool and star drag.

- Line - Monofilament is almost universal. A 10 pound test is most common for steelhead and smaller salmon. For larger salmon 20 pound line is common.

Other equipment and riggings that are needed;

- Substantial landing net(for boat anglers). Shore anglers beach their fish.

- File - to continually resharpen hooks - they get dulled on rocks, gravel, etc.

- A needle-nosed pliers - to remove hooks.

- Knife - to gut and gill fish.

- Chest high waders

- Warm clothing, a waterproof jacket and hat and polarized sun glasses.

Where to Fish

See Coastal Rivers and Valley Rivers sections.

Cleaning and Cooking

Smaller fish are filleted. Larger ones are steaked. For cooking instructions see, Catching Salmon In Oceans and Catching Trout In Streams.

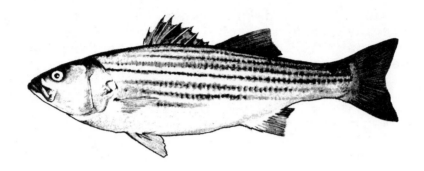

How to Catch... **Striped Bass**

One could write a book, and several people have, on the subject of striper fishing. This is the case because many techniques are used to catch stripers, depending on the location, the season of the year and the preferences in approach of different anglers. Our purpose here is to present the basics of the most successful approaches.

Striped bass were first introduced to California, from the East coast, in 1879, near Martinez. Twenty years later, the commercial catch alone was averaging well over one million pounds per year. In 1935, commercial fishing was stopped because of the dwindling population. Currently, the striper population is good, but not nearly as good as it was 20 years ago.

The life cycle of the striper is important to be aware of because it has much to do with when and where to fish. Stripers spawn in the fresh waters of the Sacramento(from Sacramento to Colusa) and San Joaquin(between the Antioch Bridge and the Middle River) Rivers from about April to mid-June. After spawning, these fish move back down into salt-water, or the brackish waters of the San Pablo and San Francisco Bays. Stripers move back up into the Delta starting

in September and these early arrivals winter over for the
spring spawn. Striped bass range in size up to 40 pounds,
or more. The average catch is probably 6-10 pounds. What
this all means, as far as where the stripers are at any
given season, is summarized in the table below;

Location	J	F	M	A	M	J	J	A	S	O	N	D
Ocean						X	X	X				
S.F. Bay						X	X	X	X	X		
Delta	X	X	X	X	X	X			X	X	X	X

The stripers habits and lifecycle, of course, are all
separate from the striper fishing that exists in several
reservoirs(e.g. San Louis, San Antonio). Impoundment populations exist because of planting programs of young stripers; or through young fish migrations through aquaducts.

Trolling

Trolling for stripers is probably the most popular
technique. It allows you to cover a fairly wide area, if
you're not sure where the fish are. Trolling is also suggested if the tides are not favorable. That is, the best
striper fishing usually occurs on a large(greater than 5.0
feet) incoming tide, after a low, low tide(say 2-3 feet, or
even minus). If these tide conditions don't exist, trolling may be the best bet.

The key to successful striper trolling is to keep
your offering near the bottom. Most often the bass are
laying close to the bottom. The most notable exception to
this is probably lake striper, where surface trolling is
often productive. Of course, the main problem with trolling on or near the bottom is snags. But many experienced
striper trollers look at losing lures to snags as part of
the cost of successful fishing. The truth is that if the
stripers are on the bottom, that's where you've got to troll

or else you'll just be wasting fuel.

Often in the Delta and Bays, the stripers are in 8-25 feet of water. In these depths it's important to get your offering well back behind the boat. The engine noise and wake spooks the fish, but if you're out far enough(say 50-140 yards) from the boat, the bass have time to return before the lure passes through their area.

The best trolling speed is 3-4mph. Once your rig is out, check the tip of your rod. It should be twitching constantly. This is the action from your lure. Adjust the boat speed to get this effect.

The rig you troll depends a lot on the depth of water you're trolling in. Use the rig that keeps your offering near the bottom. In shallow water(8-10 feet), a deep diving plug, spoon or jig can be attached directly to the line using a snap swivel. In deeper water(10-20 feet), use one of these two rigs;

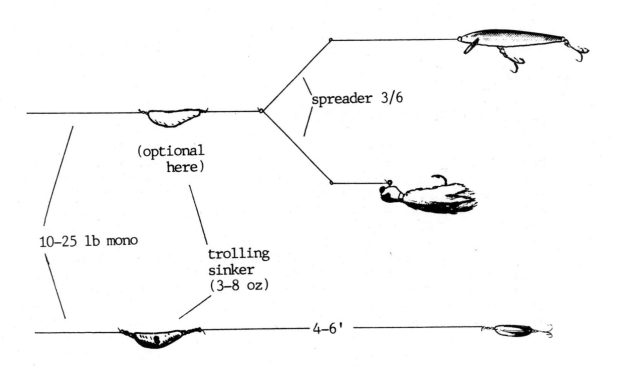

spreader 3/6

(optional here)

10-25 lb mono

trolling sinker (3-8 oz)

4-6'

Deep Troll

For this type of trolling(say in the deep water channel of the Sacramento, or San Joaquin Rivers) if this is
where your sonar tells you the fish are, you'll need to
use diving planes, lead core line or downriggers. This
type of equipment and approach is described in the Ocean
Salmon and Lake Trout and Salmon Section of this book.

The most popular trolling offerings are;

- Rebel and Rapala lures(5-6 inches, 3 treble hooks,
  jointed, deep-diving, minnow-type plugs).

- Spoons(Pet, Hopkins, Kastmaster, size 3-4 inches.

- Bug Eye Jigs(2-3 oz.) - used on short leader of
  spreader to provide depth.

Set the drag on your reel just firm enough to prevent
line from being taken out. Set the clicker in the "on"
position. A singing clicker means a strike. The trolling
action will have set the hook. Tighten down slightly on
the drag before playing the fish.

Bait Fishing

Bait fishing can be done from a boat or from shore,
although it is probably more productive from a boat(because more promising areas can be reached). As with trolling, bait fishing is best on a big changing tide. Fish
often feed on the edge of drop-offs at these times. Fish
the upstream edge on an incoming tide and the downstream
edge on an outgoing tide. The edge of a shallow flat or
sandbar is often good.

Boat anglers usually anchor and then cast out a sliding
sinker rig with a big bait hook. Stripers aren't hook shy
so a partially visible hook is no problem. The reel is left
in the free spool position. Watch the tip of your rod at all
times. Point your rod at the fish and play out 5-10 feet of

line on the slightest nibble. Next, the fish will hit hard.
Set the hook solidly by raising the rod to a vertical position quickly.

Both shore and boat anglers should use enough lead on
the rig to prevent the current from drifting it.

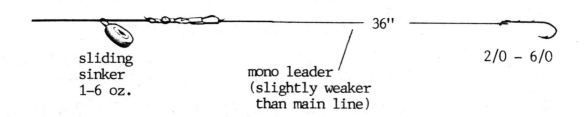

sliding
sinker
1-6 oz.

mono leader
(slightly weaker
than main line)

36"

2/0 - 6/0

Popular striped bass baits include;

. Threadfin shad

. Anchovies

. Sardines

. Shiners

. Bloodworms

. Mudsuckers

. Bullheads

. Ghost shrimp

. Grass shrimp

Local bait shops will know which are most effective
depending on location and season of the year. Live bait
fish are hooked just below the dorsal fin, with the hook
entering on one side and exiting on the other side of the
fish. Once a live bait fish dies, the hook may be put in

more securely, often with the leader secured to the tail
by a half-hitch knot. Dead bait fish are often mutilated,
or butterflied(opened vertically from throat to tail, fold-
ed over and then threaded through the curve of the hook several
times) to put blood and oil into the water. For large sardines, fillet off a side flank. Cut it in half for enough
bait for 2 hooks. For blood worms, some experts suggest
always keeping the hook tip covered with worm.

Casting

Casting for striped bass can be done from shore, from
a boat, or in the surf. In tidal waters, casting is most
productive on rapid, incoming tides. And, like largemouth
bass casting, it is often best to cast around and about
structures, such as bridge columns. Half-ounce Hair-Raisers,
Cordell Spots, and Lucky 13's are good.

In lakes, feeding birds are a key to stripers feeding
on shad near the surface. Surface plugs(shad patterns)
and half-ounce Krocodiles or Kastmasters are effective.

Surf casters also depend on the feeding birds to tip
off the location of the stripers. Common offerings are
Rebel and Rapala lures.

Surf, Drift and Pier Fishing

Surf fishing is a popular approach for taking stripers
along the Pacific coast, especially from the Golden Gate
Bridge south to Half Moon Bay. Drift fishing is used to
catch striped bass in San Francisco and San Pablo Bay. Pier
fishing at several San Francisco and San Pablo Bay piers
and particularly at Pacifica Pier, can be productive for
stripers.

Each of these three techniques is described in detail
in separate sections of this book.

Tackle and Equipment

Striper fishing can be done with a wide variety of tackle. Light weight black bass tackle can be used for casting or bait fishing. Medium weight spinning equipment, or free spool/star drag conventional reel-light action rods are used for trolling. Light spinning equipment can also be used for trolling. Some feel this is the most exciting way to take stripers in the 4-12 pound range.

Where to Fish

See San Francisco Area, San Francisco Bay and Delta maps.

Cleaning and Cooking

Smaller stripers are usually filleted. Large ones (above say 10 pounds) can be steaked.

Striped bass fillets or steaks are white, mild in flavor, low in fat and especially good eating. Barbecuing, broiling, poaching, baking and frying are all good approaches.

WHITE STURGEON

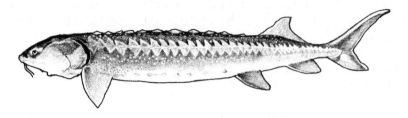

How to Catch... Sturgeon

Of the 16 species of sturgeon, two live in local waters(San Francisco Bay, San Pablo Bay, Suisun Bay, The Delta). Green sturgeon(sometimes locally referred to as yellow) are the least prevelant. Greens have long slender snouts and grow to about 7 feet in length and 350 pounds. White sturgeon(actually grey) have a more blunt nose and can grow much larger.

Fishing Techniques

Sturgeon fishing is done almost always from a boat at anchor. And the almost exclusive approach is still fishing. Because of this it's important to drop your bait in a promising location. There are prime sturgeon fishing spots throughout the Bays and Delta. Sturgeon are included in the Bays and Delta sections of this book.

Sturgeon fishing is best on a strong, incoming tide and at the turning of this tide. Most sturgeon are caught in 10-20 feet of water, often at drop-offs. Chart recorders are very helpful in locating these contours and actually "seeing" the sturgeon themselves. But, many sturgeon are caught by anglers who don't have chart recorders. Try a location. Move on in half an hour if there is no action.

Sturgeons are bottom feeders. In fact, their mouths hover over the bottom and literally suction, or vacuum in the food. So bait must be right on the bottom. Sturgeon's initial "bite" is very soft which dictates two things;

1) A sliding sinker rig.

2) A rod tip that is sensative enough to detect the light movement as the sturgeon picks up the bait and moves slightly as it suctions it in.

Many sturgeon anglers cast out or lower in their offering, tighten up the line after the bait sinks to the bottom, and then lean the rod against the transom of the boat(the rod butt on the floor). Then, when a tap is detected, the angler lifts the rod up and points the tip directly at the fish. A big pull means to set the hook hard. Several pumps are probably in order. Sturgeons have tough mouths.

Tackle and Equipment

As mentioned above a rod with a sensative tip is recommended. But, some anglers prefer heavy action rods. These also work fine, especially if the angler likes to hold the rod and sense the bite by keeping the line between the thumb and index finger. The rod should be 6½-8 feet long and have a long butt below the reel mount to lend leverage while playing the fish.

Most sturgeon anglers use conventional ocean-weight fishing reels. But, relatively heavy spinning reels with a good drag and the capability to hold 250 yards or so of 30 pound line will also work.

A landing net will work for sturgeon that are only a foot or more over the legal limit(40 inches). Beyond this a gaff or snair is probably required.

Bait and Rigging

Two or three hook sturgeon rigs can be purchased at many Bay area bait shops. 6/0 size hooks are recommended. These leaders use wire line. Attach the rig to your line with a strong snap swivel.

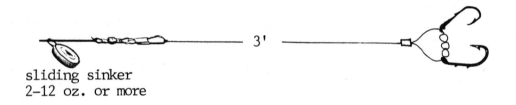

sliding sinker
2-12 oz. or more

Grass shrimp are the most common bait. Mud and ghost shrimp are also used. Two people need about 1 pound of bait. Load up each hook with bait. 4 or 5 shrimps may be needed. The bigger the wad the better. Live or fresh bait is most desirable. You can slide shrimp up the hook leader. Some suggest putting shrimp on the hook, tail first.

Anchovies and clams can also be used for bait. Some use a small hair net to hold these baits in a glob.

Where to Fish

See San Francisco Bay and Delta Sections.

Cleaning and Cooking

The first item on the agenda is to gut the fish. Next, slice off the sharp spines along the sides, top and bottom. Slice through the skin on the back and belly and along the rear of the gill cage. By hand, or with a pair of pliers, pull the skin off each side. Now, cut off the head and make a deep cut around the fish right in front of the tail. You can now remove the spinal column in one piece. Finally, steak the fish and fillet the tail section. Trim off the red meat along the sides and next to the spinal column.

Sturgeon can be cooked in many ways. Baked or barbecued, lightly floured and pan-fried in butter, or smoked. The flesh is lean, compact, almost meat-like and quite rich.

BROWN TROUT

How to Catch...Trout(in Streams)

We are blessed by the numerous, fine trout streams in Northern California(see page 179).   Stream trout fishing is appealing because it can be the type of experience you personally want it to be. It can be accessible or remote, challenging or relaxing, simple or complicated.

Many people have a stereotype in their minds of the typical trout angler. It includes a flyrod, hip-high waders, a vest decorated with multicolored flys, a hat with more multicolored flys, a landing net hanging from the waist, all topped off with a Norman Rockwell-like wicker creel. This, of course, exactly describes some trout fishermen. But, forget this stereotype. Stream trout fishing can be productive and enjoyable, not only for the avid, well-equiped fly fisherman, but for everyone. You don't even need to use a flyrod, if you don't want to.

The purpose of this section is to describe, in detail, several of the basic ways to catch stream trout, regardless of the type of fishing you prefer and the type of tackle you have.

There are several different types of trout in Northern

Califronia streams. The most common are rainbow. Most are planted, but some are native. Others include the German brown trout and the brook trout.

Some Fundamentals

Stream trout fishing, no matter what equipment is used, focuses on casting a fly, spinner, spoon, or bait into a likely place in the stream and then retrieving it in as natural a manner as possible.

Other fundamentals;

- Trout always face upstream, watching for food to be delivered to them by the moving water. So your offering should be presented in the same manner - moving from upstream to downstream.

- Trout are very leary and easily spooked. Since they're facing upstream and smelling the water that comes from upstream, always move upstream as you fish. This way, you're less likely to be detected. Move quietly and stay out of the line of sight of likely trout hangouts.

- In the same vane, fish on the shady side of the stream, especially in the hours just after sunrise and just before sunset.

- Casts in an upstream direction or up and across the stream are preferred over downstream casts. Downstream casts require a retrieve that is against the current and therefore, unnatural in appearances.

- Trout stay near the bottom of the stream. So your offering must move along near the bottom. The exception to this rule is when dry fly fishing. Dry fly(floating flys) imitate floating insects being carried along by the current. Trout will rise up to take these flys. Dry fly fishing is evening fishing.

- As with most fishing, early mornings and evening are best fishing periods. But, trout can
  be caught at any time of day.

- Keep hooks sharp. Banging rocks and pebbles can
  dull them quickly.

- If you're not succeeding in whatever approach
  you're using(flys, spinners, bait), try other
  offerings until you find the one that works.

- Trout hang out behind boulders that break the
  current, in deep holes, in slower water near
  the undercut edge of a stream(especially in sha-
  ded areas), and at the head and tail of pools.
  Concentrate your efforts on these areas.

- When you spot an obviously expert trout angler,
  watch where he or she casts from and where he
  or she put the offering and how it is retrieved.

- Often the best places to cast from are in the
  water. Don't let that stop you. Just be careful and carry a wading staff to probe the bottom
  and improve balance.

Fly Fishing

Flys, both dry(floating) and wet(sinking) are very
small and light. Too light to cast any distance. In fly
fishing this difficulty is overcome by using flyline that
has enough weight so it can be cast. The fly, connected
by a light leader to the end of the flyline "just goes
along for a ride" as the line is played out and finally
set on its final trajectory. The purpose of the fly reel
is simply to store line that is not being used, at the
moment, and to retrieve line when necessary.

Fly fishing is an art and a science. Some say it is the ultimate fishing experience. Some people only fly fish. Many whole volumes have been written on fly fishing. In our limited space here we cannot compete. But here are the insights that produce fish in Northern California.

. If you're having trouble handling fly fishing equipment and making a good cast, consider a fly fishing class, watch others do it, read up on the subject in specialized books, and practice, practice, practice.

. Dry flys must float. Floating solution, leader sinking solution, tapered leaders and generally good floating fly line make this possible.

. As the old truism goes, "match the hatch." Dry flys must imitate nature. Good Northern California dry flys include Mosquito, Light Cahill and Dark Hendrickson. Size # 14 and #16 are best.

. Present the dry fly above the suspected feeding fish and let it float naturally through that feeding area.

. Dry fly fishing is an evening affair. The several hours before dark are best.

. Wet flys imitate underwater creatures such as the larve or pupa state of aquatic insects, nymphs, grubs, etc.

. Successful wet flys in Northern California include #6 and #8 bee imitation, wet moss imitation, brown or black spent wing flys and light tan caddis larve fly.

. As the fly drifts back to you, take in excessive line. Then you'll be ready to strike. This is also true in dry fly fishing.

. Watch the tip of your floating fly line. If it hesitates or pauses, set the hook.

. Many wet fly devotees use two different
  flys at a time.

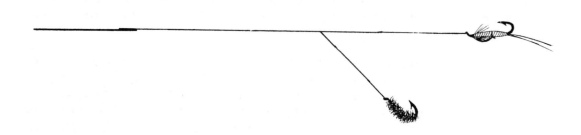

There is a great deal of variety in fly fishing
equipment. One can spend hundreds of dollars or you can
buy a rod/reel combination that is quite decent for less
than $50.00. For starters, a 7½ to 8½ foot rod matched with
number six line is good. An automatic reel costs a few
dollars more, but makes taking up excessive line so much
easier.

Spinning

Spinning fishing means stream trout fishing using
spinning or even spincasting equipment. The most popular set-ups include light spinning tackle and ultra-
light spinning tackle. Ultra-light tackle is the easiest
to handle and probably the most appropriate. It's capable of casting even small offerings, to sufficient dis-
tances with a 4 pound test line. Here are the fundamentals of stream trout fishing with spinning tackle;

. The most common lures are very small spinners,
  probably never larger than a #2. Since retrieves are with the current(you're still casting upstream), a spinner whose blade rotates
  freely with little more motion than current
  speed is most desirable. These spinners imitate swimming bait fish. A popular example of

a spinner of this caliber is the Panther Mar-
tin #2, 1/16 oz. black bodied spinner. Gold
blades are good for low light or overcast periods, chrome blades are recommended for sunny
periods, and copper is good for not-so-clear
water. Try several.

. Besides spinners, spoons are also good, like
the Super Duper. Retreival speed is critical
for the success of both spinners and spoons.
Test both in quiet pools. Both types put out
a vibration that can be sensed in the motion
at the tip of the rod . Watch for this and adjust retrieval speed accordingly. Also, frequently change return speed to give offerings
a more natural swimming pattern.

. Spinners need to be worked near the bottom.
Adjust your retrieval speed to achieve this.
You'll hang up some spinners, but you'll catch
more fish.

. Some lures are best tied directly to the main
line. Others may twist the line if a small snap-
swivel is not used. Experiment, but if using
a swivel, make sure it is in good working order
and has a rounded connector at the lure end.
This will insure proper action in the water.

Bait

   Stream trout fishing with bait is the most flexible
of all approaches. It's flexible because of the wide
choice of bait that produce fish. And it's flexible because it can be done with either fly fishing equipment or
spinning equipment. Some devotees even combine the two
by using monofilament line on a fly rod/reel. All these
possibilities are fine. Here are the fundamentals of
trout stream bait fishing;

   . Redworms are probably the most popular bait
followed by bottled salmon eggs. Cheese and
marshmallows are also popular. Then, there is

a whole category of natural, live baits including crickets, beetles, grubs, larvae and pupae. Some anglers collect bait right out of the stream by using a fine mesh screen to trap bait dislodged by moving large rocks in the streambeds.

. If you're using live bait, it should be alive. So, store and transport them carefully and hook them so as not to inflict fatal damage(at least not instant fatal damage).

. A short shank #8 or #10 hook is good. Try to conceal the entire hook into the bait.

. You want the bait to drift along with the current near the bottom of the stream. Unweighted drifting is best. If you need weight to get near the bottom, use as little split shot as possible, about 8" to 10" from the hook.

. Since your bait is under water and drifting, it's not all that easy to detect bites. It helps to keep slack out of the line(while still allowing drift) and to set the hook on any sign of hesitation or pause in drift.

Casting Bobber

Purest fly fishermen may cringe at this approach, but here goes anyway. Some people would like to be able to cast flys or small baits without mastering a fly rod. And some can't afford fly fishing equipment. For this group, a casting bobber is the answer.

A casting bobber is a small, clear plastic float that adds enough weight to a fly or a small bait to allow casting with a spinning or spincasting reel and monofilament line.

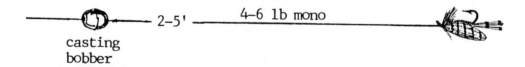

casting
bobber

2-5'   4-6 lb mono

Casting bobbers are available in several sizes and configurations. Some even allow you to vary weight by allowing water inside the bobber.

Fish a casting bobber rig just as you would a dry fly. If you use a wet fly or bait, allow enough distance between the bobber and the hook so your offering gets down to near the bottom. In rapidly flowing water, some split shot about 8 inches from the hook may be added.

Tackle and Equipment

Besides your choice of rod and reel, line and entice-ments to put at the end of it, trout anglers need several other items. Essential are both a creel(canvas ones can be purchased for as little as $5.00) or a fishing vest and an inexpensive landing net. A needle-nose pliers or other hook removing device is also essential. Small trout should be released, with as little hook damage as possible. In fact, some trout fishermen flatten the barbs on all their hooks to facilitate catch and release. Releasing large trout is possibly even more important. It takes large ones to produce small ones.

Optional equipment for trout fishing includes pola-rized sun glasses, waders and a wading staff. The sun glasses help take the glare off the water and improve under-water visibility. The use of waders depends on air temper-ature, water temperature, the number of stepping stones in a stream and ones desire to stay dry. Wading staffs(just a light tree limb) are great to help maintain balance.

Cleaning and Cooking

Small trout(pan size) are generally just gutted and gilled(field cleaned). Larger trout are often filleted.

Trout is mild, lean and sweet. It is suitable for just about any cooking approach. Sauteing is probably the most popular.

110

EAGLE LAKE RAINBOW TROUT

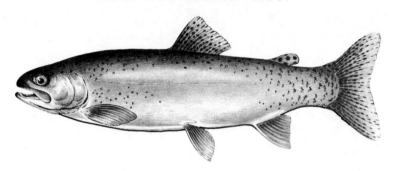

How to Catch...Trout and Salmon(in Lakes)

Fishing for trout in lakes is very different from stream trout fishing. This is true because the lake environment changes the behavior of trout. Stream trout are always facing upstream, confined to shallow waters, on or near the bottom, and near or behind structures like boulders, undercuts, etc. The stream determines the location and habits of trout.

Trout in lakes have different groundrules dictating their lives. Food doesn't necessarily "flow" to them, they must find it. Lake water temperatures vary by season and depth, so trout will change depth to find oxygen-rich water of a comfortable temperature for them. At times they may be near the surface, and at other times they may be down 80 feet or more.

Some of Northern California trout lakes also have king or silver salmon planted in them. Salmon and trout in lakes behave and are caught using the same techniques, lures and bait. Usually, anglers pursuing trout will catch an occassional salmon.

If you're catching trout in a lake, especially in the

summertime, and you'd like some salmon, it sometimes helps
to fish a little deeper. Research has shown that rainbow
and brown trout favor water temperatures of between 55° and
60°. But, the same research determined that king and silver
salmon favor 55° water, which will be down deeper.

Reading a Lake

The specifics of a lake says a lot about the location
of trout. And, as many anglers have discovered, you've
got to find them before you can catch them. As a matter
of fact, catching trout in lakes is quite easy, once they
are located. Here are the fundamentals;

. Trout, even in lakes, relate to structures.
Trout use structures to shelter themselves
from predators and to keep out of direct sun.
Depending on the time of year, overhanging trees,
cliff areas, submerged points, coves and submerged river channels are good starting points.

. Trout move to locate food and oxygen. The primary inlet to a lake is always a prime location.
It washes in food and cool, oxygen-rich water.
In cooler months, shoreline weedbeds may also
provide insects and bait fish. The windward
shoreline is also a good possibility. Drifting food will concentrate here. Finally, newly
planted trout usually hang around the planting
site for several days or more.

. A depth sounder can be an important tool. It
not only will locate structure-like underwater
islands and submerged drop-offs, but it will
also locate schools of bait fish and the trout
or salmon themselves.

. Most Northern California lakes stratify(or divide) into three layers during spring, and remain
in this condition until fall. The top layer is
too warm and too low in oxygen for trout and
salmon. They concentrate near the top of the
second layer, or thermocline. In this layer
there is planty of oxygen and forage fish. This

layer may be from 15 to 50 feet down depending on lake depth and size. Water temperature
will be in the 55-60° range. A depth sounder,
underwater temperature gauge or locals can all
help you to determine the proper depth to fish.

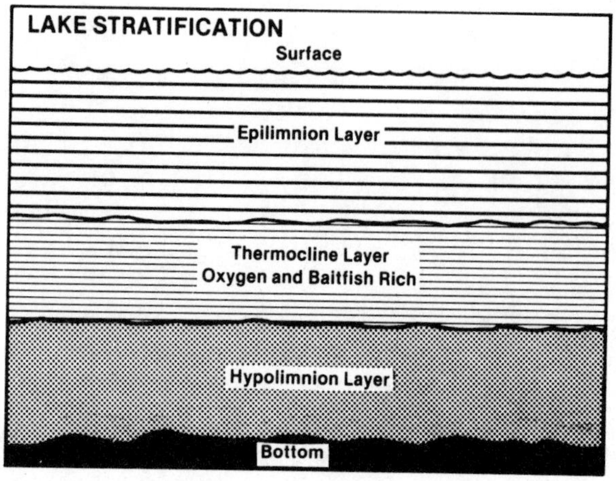

LAKE STRATIFICATION
Surface

Epilimnion Layer

Thermocline Layer
Oxygen and Baitfish Rich

Hypolimnion Layer

Bottom

Fishing Techniques

There are three primary methods of catching trout in
lakes;

1. Trolling - In one form or another, this is
    probably the most productive method of catch-
    ing trout in most lakes.

2. Bait Fishing - A very good method, especially
    for shore fishing.

3. Casting - Also a very productive shore fishing
    method. Can also be done from a boat.

It is also possible to catch trout in lakes by fly
fishing. But, even avid fly fishermen will admit it is

difficult. Dry flies will only work, for example, when an
insect hatch is taking place. Even then, they may not work
because they don't move with the current as they do in
streams. Wet flies, streamers, etc., can be used in lakes,
and can produce at times, if you're either very skillful or
very lucky. If you're interested in these techniques, check
out several fly fishing books from your local public library.

Trolling

Trolling is simply pulling an offering at the end of
your line, through the water, using a boat. It can and is
done with boats ranging from a canoe, to a rowboat, to an
inboard/outboard.

There are actually two separate and distinct aspects
of trolling for trout. The first is the trolling rig itself, and the second is the tackle/equipment combinations
used to troll the rig at a prescribed depth. Let's look
at each separately;

Trolling Rig - A trolling rig is made up of these
components(in order of placement on line);

1. Rudder - A blade to prevent line twist.

2. Flasher - An attractant which imitates a
   school of bait fish.

3. Swivel - Prevents twist.

4. Snubber - Absorbs shock of a strike. Use is
   optional, but recommended.

5. Leader - About 18" of monofilament.

6. Offering - Spoon, plug or baited hook.

The flasher and rudder are usually sold in a packaged
unit. Use larger units for murky water or deep trolling.
Then you just attach on the snubber, tie on a leader and
attach your offering. See next page for diagram.

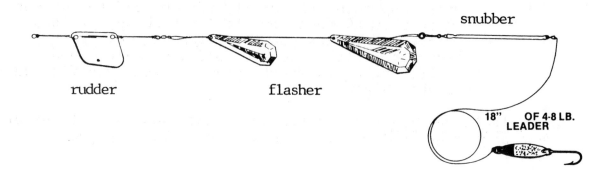

Trolling Tackle/Equipment - Unlike the trolling rig, which is quite standard, trolling tackle/equipment provides several options and alternatives.

When a lake has not stratified and trout are found near the surface trolling rigs can be handled with light spinning or baitcasting tackle and about 10-12 pound monofilament line. Weight can be added to the rudder(using tied line) to troll 2-10 feet down below the surface. Sometimes a flasher is not used.

Unfortunately, we all do most of our lake trout fishing when the trout are down in the thermocline. This presents similar problems to ocean trolling for salmon. And the alternative solutions are similar.

To get a trolling rig down to 40 or 80 or 120 feet you have these choices;

   . Use leadcore trolling line on a good sized conventional reel. Medium Penn freshwater reels with levelwind are popular(e.g. 210 series). With a slow trolling speed, leadcore line sinks at about 45°, so, for example, 50 feet of line, will produce 25 foot trolling depth.

   . Use a diving plane(see descriptions in ocean salmon section).

. Use a downrigger - This is by far the most desirable approach, especially if you need to go down
more than 40 feet, but it isn't cheap. A downrigger will take your trolling rig down to a
known depth(they're equipped with depth coun-
ters) and allow you to play and land the fish on
light tackle.

Trolling Tips - No matter what depth you're trolling or
what equipment you're using, these tips will help produce
fish;

. Troll slowly. The best trolling is slow trolling.
Some highly successful trollers, for example, use
only oar power.

. Change trolling speed often. Every minute or two
isn't too frequent. Sometimes it even helps to
speed up for just a few seconds and then slow
down. This gives added up-and-down action to
the flasher and lure.

. Change depth. If you're not sure of the depth
you're trolling at(it can vary depending on
boat speed and amount of line out, for all
approaches except downrigging) or the depth the
trout are at, vary depth until you get a strike.
Then stick there.

. Troll an "S" pattern. Trolling experts suggest
this approach 1)because it covers more territory
than straight line trolling and 2)because it
causes speed, direction and depth changes to occur
in the flasher and lure. These movements and resulting vibrations attract trout.

Bait

Bait fishing can be done from shore or boat. The most
common tackle is light spinning equipment.

Despite all the variety in trout bait fishing, the most
productive technique is probably the sliding sinker rig. It

is most often used from shore, but also is well suited to anchored boat fishing in coves and inlets.

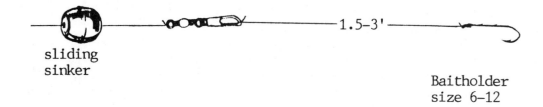

sliding
sinker

1.5-3'

Baitholder
size 6-12

The purpose of the sliding sinker rig is to allow the bait to move freely when a trout picks it up. With a fixed sinker rig, the trout would notice the drag on the offering and drop it.

The process begins by casting out the baited rig to a likely spot. Let it sink all the way to the bottom. Point the tip of your rod towards the water and slowly crank in any slack. Now, sit down, get comfortable and open the bail on your spinning reel. Personally, I don't believe in putting a rod down or propping it up on a stick. I believe in holding the rod. Then you can feel the slightest tug on your bait. In fact, I like to have my line, in front of the reel, go between the thumb and index finger of my non-reeling hand. This puts my senses directly in touch with my bait.

When the trout picks up the bait, play off line from the spool, so no resistance is felt by the fish. A pause may be detected after the first movement of line. Wait until it starts moving out again(this means the trout has swallowed the bait, literally swallowed the bait). Close the bail and set the hook. You've got yourself a fish.

A wide variety of baits are used. Salmon eggs, cheese, minnows, shad, worms, crickets. A combination of baits is also popular. Some use a small marshmallow/salmon egg/night-crawler combination. The egg provides visual attraction and the marshmallow provides buoyancy so the whole offering floats slightly off the bottom. Another way to accomplish this buoyant effect using nightcrawlers is to inflate them with air. Crawler inflaters are available to accomplish this task. Many large trout are caught on both combination baits and inflated nightcrawlers.

Bobber fishing can also be quite effective for trout. This is an especially effective method in winter and early spring when lake surface temperatures are cool and trout are often feeding near the surface. Simply tie your hook to the line, put a split shot a foot or so up from the hook, and snap on a bobber up the line. Six feet is a good distance to try first. Cast it out and watch your bobber.

Casting

Casting for trout is a popular shore fishing option, especially among younger anglers. And it can be effective. The most popular tackle is again light spinning or spincasting.

Lures can be tied directly to the end of the main line or attached with a snap swivel. I prefer the snap swivel. It prevents any line twist and provides a way to change lures easily. Most trout lures imitate small bait fish. Silver and gold colors are good in 1/8 to 3/8 oz. sizes;

- Kastmasters

- Roostertails

- Pheobes

- Mepps Spinners

Cast out as far as possible, let lure settle and return at speed that provides the most natural action. Slower is probably better. And vary the pace of your retrieve. The small bait you're trying to duplicate don't swim fast and they don't swim at a steady pace. Sometimes it's best to let the lure sink for sometime before starting your retrieve. A problem with this approach is the frequent snags(on sunken branches, etc.) and lost lures. Some anglers minimize this difficulty by replacing the original treble hook with a weedless hook.

Cleaning and Cooking

See Trout(Stream) Section.

Surf Fishing

I always think of William Conrad, casting into the surf at sunset on a beautiful Pacific beach, when I think of surf fishing. He starts his outdoor program on T.V. with this scene, year after year. And why not? Surf fishing is man and nature at its best. It's just you, the roaring breakers, the sea birds, and salt spray and hopefully the fish.

Tackle and Equipment

Surf anglers are of two types. The most aggressive are the cast and retrieve people. They cast plugs and spoons that weigh 2-4 oz. into the surf and then retrieve them, alert for a striper or occassional salmon strike. Halibut can also be taken. Surf casters typically use a two-hand grip rod of about 10 feet in length. A shorter rod lacks the needed distance, while a longer one is slower and more difficult to control. Bait anglers prefer a longer rod, to keep their line up out of the breaker tops. They cast out a rig consisting of a 2-4 oz. pyramid sinker at the end of a leader that has 2 or 3 hooks. These rigs are available in most stores for a very reasonable price.

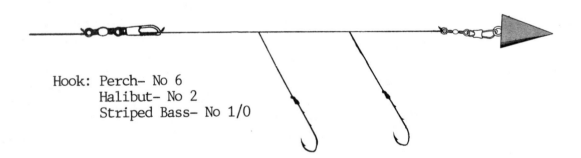

Hook: Perch- No 6
      Halibut- No 2
      Striped Bass- No 1/0

They then set the pole in a sandspike rodholder and wait for a bite from most likely a perch or kingfish, or an occassional flounder or striped bass. Stripers are most often caught by casters and the several varieties of perch by bait anglers. By far, most surf anglers use spinning reels - both casters and bait anglers. A reel

like the Garcia Cardinal 700 with rear drag is popular.
The reel used should hold 200 to 250 yards of 15-30 test
monofilament line. Conventional reels with a free spool
and star drag(like the Penn Squidder) are for tradition-
alists who have mastered the art of thumbing the spool to
prevent backlash.

The only other equipment needed is a large bucket
(for fish) and waders or wetsuit bottoms.

Fishing Techniques

Bait anglers use bloodworms, pileworms, sand crabs and
anchovies. Effective offerings for casters include Pencil-
Poppers, Zara Spooks, Hopkins No-Eql, Krocodiles, Kastmasters and bucktail and bugeye jigs.

Where on a beach one fishes is important. It's best
to scout a beach at low tide. Steeply sloping beaches are
best. Look for holes and channels where the surf is not
breaking. When the tide floods in, these become the feeding
grounds for fish. The rising tide up to high tide and an
hour or two after are usually the best times to fish.

Striper anglers watch for birds like gulls, sheerwaters,
pelicans or cormorants diving into the surf in pursuit of
bait fish. These bait fish are driven into the beach by
stripers feeding. These birds are the casters main clue
as to when the stripers are feeding and in which direction
they may be moving. The key is to cast the line where the
bait fish are and to retrieve it so it duplicates a wounded
baitfish. Early mornings and dusk are often the best time
to use the birds as trackers.

Where to Fish

Actually any accessible surf has the potential of
being a good surf fishing location. But, some locations
are more accessible and have developed a reputation as
productive fishing stretches. Starting from the Oregon

border and working south, here is a list of some of the best;

. North of Humbolt: Prairie Creek Redwood
State Park, Trinidad State Beach, Mad River
Beach Couty Park

. Humbolt Bay: North Spit(take Hwy: 225),
South Spit(take Table Bluff Road)

. Mendocino County: MacKerricher State Park,
Manchester State Beach

. Sonoma County: coast state beaches north
of Bodega Bay

. Marin County: Point Reyes National Sea-
shore(north and south beaches), Stinson
Beach

. San Francisco City & County: Baker Beach,
Ocean Beach, Fleishhacker Beach

. San Mateo County: Thornton State Beach
Mussel Rock, Sharp Park State Beach, Rock-
away Beach, Linda Mar Beach, Monata State
Beach, Half Moon Bay State Beaches

. Monterey Bay: Twin Lakes, New Brighton,
Seacliff, Sunset and Moss Landing State
Beaches. Carmel River State Beach

Drift Fishing

Here's another instance of a confusing name. As used in San Francisco Bay waters, drift fishing means fishing from a drifting boat over productive areas(reefs, drop-offs). Water movement and wind move the boat with the engine used just to position the boat to start a drift(or correct it).

Drift fishing is included in this section rather than in the Striped Bass Section of this book because this technique is useful for more than stripers. Halibut, rockfish, lingcod, sharks and even salmon, at times, are caught this way.

Tackle and Equipment

Drift fishing tackle is quite basic. Most anglers use a 6-7 foot boat rod with a sensitive tip(to detect bites), a conventional saltwater reel loaded with 25-30 pound test monofilament line. Reel line capacity should be in the 200-300 yard range.

Terminal tackle is also straightforward. Here's the setup;

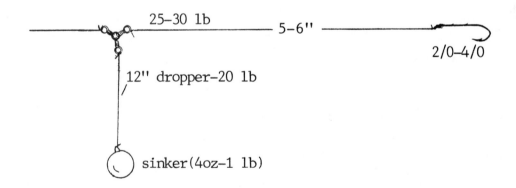

Sinker size depends on current speed. An 8 oz. cannonball sinker is most common but in a fast current, up to a pound is needed to keep the rig in contact with the bottom.

How To

San Francisco Bay drift fishing is actually a second cousin to open ocean bottom fishing. In both instances, the idea is to drift over structures, while keeping the rig on the bottom but without getting snagged too frequently. The terminal tackle is different because live anchovies are the bait of choice(most ocean bottom fishing is done with cut pieces of squid or anchovies). Most anglers bait the anchovies up through both lips – not too deep or the bait life and effectiveness will be diminished.

Lower the baited rig until you feel bottom. Then, take up slack and actually lift the weight off the bottom a reel turn or two. Now, by raising and lowering the rod tip, or even by reeling in or letting out a little line, the key is to stay in contact with the bottom without getting hung up. Gently lower the weight to the bottom every few seconds to make sure your offering is still close. Remember, the fish are feeding near structures. You want your bait to be there too. Don't lapse into daydreaming or just drag your weight along the bottom. Rather, try to imagine the shape of the bottom as you drift over it. Try to picture its shape. "Feel" the bottom and its changing depth and adjust your depth accordingly.

Where to Fish

Some of the prime drift fishing locations in San Francisco Bay are listed below(see NOAA Nautical Chart 18652- which you should have on board for safe boating on San Francisco Bay);

. Alcatraz Island – south side

. Arch Rock

. Blossom Rock

. Buoy #8

- Harding Rock

- Lime Point and Yellow Bluff - off Marin

- Peanut Farm

- Point Bonita

- Raccoon Straits

- Shag Rock

- Sharks Point

- South Tower of Golden Gate Bridge

- Treasure Island and Pier 21 - north and east of
  island

Pier Fishing

People who don't know about pier(or wharf) fishing think it's just for kids. But kids of all ages enjoy pier fishing. It's a way to fish in the big waters without seasickness, a boat, or party boat fees. A minimum amount of equipment is required, but the opportunities for choice fish are there. Pier anglers catch 5, 10, or even 20 pound fish. They catch salmon, striped bass, halibut, rockfish, lingcod, flounder, sharks, rays, sanddabs, bonita, mackeral, steelhead, kingfish, perch and sharks.

Tackle and Equipment

Any type of rod and reel made has been used by pier anglers but since we're talking good-sized fish, tackle should be hefty enough for the fish being sought. For a 10-15 pound fish(like nice striper, salmon or halibut) use a medium to medium heavy rod(6-8 feet), a reel capable of holding a 100 yards of 10-25 pound line that has a decent drag system (either spinning or conventional). For bottom fishing you can use a rockfish rig or a striper rig(see these sections for details). Bobbers are also used to drift bait. Popular baits include anchovies, squid, clams, pileworms and blood-worms.

Other things you'll need are a big pail(for your catch), a long piece of clothesline, and a crab net. The net is used to raise-up good-sized fish from the water line to the pier level. Have a fellow angler operate the net and be sure the fish is tired-out before netting and raising it.

Fishing Techniques

Still fishing is the most popular approach, but casting can also be productive. Salmon, striper and halibut can be taken this way. Use the same lure that bait trollers use (see those specific sections).

Timing is all important to successful pier fishing. Since we can't take the pier to the fish, we've got to go to the pier when the fish are there. And, most fish are not there most of the time. They come and go, often in as little as several days or several weeks. This is where local, timely information is essential. Keep in frequent telephone contact with local bait shops, rangers, or outdoor writers. When the salmon, striper, or halibut are there, go after them.

At many piers, tide movements can also effect the bite. A large swing in tides(a large difference between high and low tide) marks a good day to fish and just before, during and after high tide is a good time. But, this isn't always so. Some days the fish are just there and biting no matter what, especially if the bait fish are near the pier.

Where to Fish

Here are some of the most popular fishing piers in Northern California;

ANTIOCH - Take highway 4 eastbound to Antioch Bridge. Take the Wilbur Avenue off-ramp just before the toll plaza. Follow the frontage road to the pier which is just to the right of the bridge.

ANTIOCH - Located at the foot of "H" Street in Antioch.

BERKELEY FISHING PIER - City of Berkeley. Highway 80 to University off-ramp, follow the signs to the Berkeley Marina. The pier is at the foot of Univeristy Avenue, just past the bait shop and marina.

POINT BENECIA FISHING PIER - Located in Solano County.

BRISBANE FISHING PIER - Off highway 101, 2.5 miles south of San Francisco city limit.

CANDLESTICK PARK PUBLIC PIER - Located south of Candlestick Park, off Hunter's Point Expressway and Jamestown Avenue.

CAPITOLA FISHING WHARF - Take Bay Avenue exit off Hwy 1 and follow to Capitola Village.

CHINA CAMP PIER - Located at China Camp State Park. Take north San Pedro off-ramp from Hwy. 101 near Marin County Civic Center and proceed east approximately four miles.

EMERYVILLE FISHING PIER - City of Emeryville. Take the Powell Street Exit from Hwy. 80 to Emeryville. Travel west on Powell Street to its end in the Emeryville Marina. The pier is at the foot of Powell Street.

FORT MASON PIERS - Golden Gate National Recreation Area. Located in the northern end of Fort Mason, off Marina Blvd., San Francisco.

FORT POINT PIER - Golden Gate National Recreation Area. Located near Fort Point in the Presidio. From Hwy. 101 near the Golden Gate Bridge toll plaza, take the view roads to Lincoln Blvd., then to Battery E Road to the pier.

FRUITVALE BRIDGE PARK - City of Oakland. Take SR 17 to the High Street exit. From High Street turn onto Alameda Avenue and travel west to the intersection with Fruitvale Avenue. The pier is on the southeast shore of the Oakland Estuary next to the Fruitvale Bridge.

MARINA GREEN JETTY - Located in San Francisco, at the end of East Harbor. Take Marina Blvd., to Gashouse Cove and then to East Harbor.

MARTINEZ FISHING PIER - Martinez Marina; take Hwy. 4 to Alhambra off-ramp. Travel through Martinez to the end of the road. Follow signs to the parking area and pier.

MIDDLE HARBOR PARK - City of Oakland. Take SR 17 to Oakland. If travelling south, take the Cypress Street exit and follow it west to the intersection with Seventh Street. Turn left and continue south to the intersection of Adeline St. Turn right onto Adeline and continue west. Adeline turns into Middle Harbor Road. Continue on Middle Harbor to the intersection with Ferro St., near the Middle Harbor Terminal. Turn left onto Ferro Street and follow it around the terminal on the Oakland Estuary. If travelling north, take the Oak Street exit, turn right onto Oak Street, travel one block east, and turn left onto Seventh Street and travel north to the intersection of Adeline Street. Proceed on Adeline, as above.

MISSION ROCK PIER - San Francisco; located at Agua Vista Park, off China Basin, near Mission Rock Resort.

MONTEREY MUNICIPAL WHARF - In Monterey, at Fisherman's Wharf.

MUNICIPAL PIER - City of San Francisco. Located at the foot of Van Ness Avenue.

PACIFICA PIER - Located in Pacifica. Entry from Beach Blvd. and Santa Rosa. Extends into the ocean from Sharp Park State Beach.

PARADISE PIER - Marin County Parks and Recreation. Vehicle entry fee collected on weekends. From Hwy. 101 near Mill Valley, take Tiburon off-ramp and proceed on Paradise Drive to the pier.

POINT PINOLE - East Bay Regional Park District. From Interstate 80 take the Hilltop exit in Richmond. Proceed west on Hilltop to the intersection with San Pablo Avenue. Turn right onto San Pablo Avenue and proceed north to the intersection with Atlas Road. Turn left onto Atlas. Take the park shuttle bus or walk to pier.

SEACLIFF PIER - In Seacliff Beach State Park, just south of Capitola.

TWENTY-FOURTH STREET PIER - Located at the east end on 24th street in San Francisco near the P.G.&E. plant.

WERDER PIER-FOSTER CITY - Located at the end of Hillsdale Blvd. next to the Highway 92 Bridge.

PITTSBURG - Take Hwy. 4 to Railroad Avenue. Head north until you reach the city marina. Turn left ½ block and follow the road to the parking area.

SAN LEANDRO FISHING PIER - Take SR 17 to Marina Blvd. exit in San Leandro. Travel west on Marina to an intersection with Neptune Drive. Turn left onto San Leandro Marina and Marina. The pier is on South Dike Rd. in the marina.

SANTA CRUZ MUNICIPAL WHARF - Located right by the Boardwalk in downtown Santa Cruz.

Fishing Regulations

Regulations for the fish covered in this book are displayed below. This information is current as of this printing. For any modifications, exceptions, and trout and salmon regulations, see current California Sport Fishing Regulations—A Summary, available free at your local tackle or bait dealer.

Species	Season	Limit	Minimum Size(inches)
Abalone	April – June and August – November(north of Yankee Pt.near Monterey); ½ hr. before sunrise to ½ hr. after sunset	4 in combination	Black-5 Green, pink, white-6 Red-7 All other-4
Albacore	All year	none	none
Black Bass -largemouth -smallmouth	All year	5	12*
Catfish	All year	20*	None
Crayfish	All year	None	None
Halibut, California	All year	5*	22
Kokanee	**	**	**
Lingcod	All year	5	22
Panfish	All year	None	None
Rock Cod	All year	15	None
Rock Crabs	All year	35	4" across widest part of back***
Salmon(in ocean)	Mid February-Mid November*	2	20*
Salmon (inland)	**	**	**
Shad	All year	25	None
Shark	All year	None	None
Steelhead	**	**	**
Stripes Bass	All year	3*	16*
Sturgeon	All year	1	40
Trout	**	**	**

* – See regulations for exceptions

** – See trout and salmon regulations

*** – Rock crabs have distinctive black marking on the tips of their pincers. Crab without these markings are probably Dungeness. See regulations.

LAKE FISHING

Lake Almanor

Lake Almanor is one of the best trout and salmon fishing lakes in California. Trout include native rainbow, browns and Eagle Lake rainbow. King(chinook) salmon fishing is excellent. Almanor also provides bass(both large-mouth and smallmouth), catfish and panfish angling. This is a large lake(about 13 miles long and 6 miles wide) that has excellent facilities including campgrounds(PG&E), as well as numerous resorts and marinas. Although Almanor is at 4500 feet altitude, the lakes surface temperature in summer is about 70°.

Fishing Seasons (+=good, -=fair)

Species	J	F	M	A	M	J	J	A	S	O	N	D
Trout	+	+	+	+	-	-	-	-	-	-	+	+
Salmon	+	+	+	+	-	-	-	-	-	-	+	+
Bass				-	+	+	+	+	+	+	-	
Catfish				-	-	-	-	-	-	-	-	

Fishing Tips

The most productive technique for trout and salmon at Almanor is trolling. During summer when the lake is stratified, trolling is consistently best down 30-35 feet. Shore fishing is also good. The cove just west of the dam produces trout, salmon and smallmouth bass. The PG&E campground at Rocky Point(about a mile up from the dam) is good for trout and bass. A year around favorite shore fishing location is in Hamilton Branch, where the stream enters the lake. A popular still fishing location, requiring a boat, is Big Spring Cove at Hamilton Branch. Favorite still fishing baits are salmon eggs, nightcrawlers, and salmon roe.

Information/Bait/Tackle

There are numerous sources for fishing information, bait and tackle at Lake Almanor. Many of the resorts and marinas, as well as several sporting goods stores are anxious to provide information and supplies.

Marinas and Launch Ramps

Lake Almanor has over a dozen marinas and launch ramps, most located in the eastern portion and southern portion of the lake.

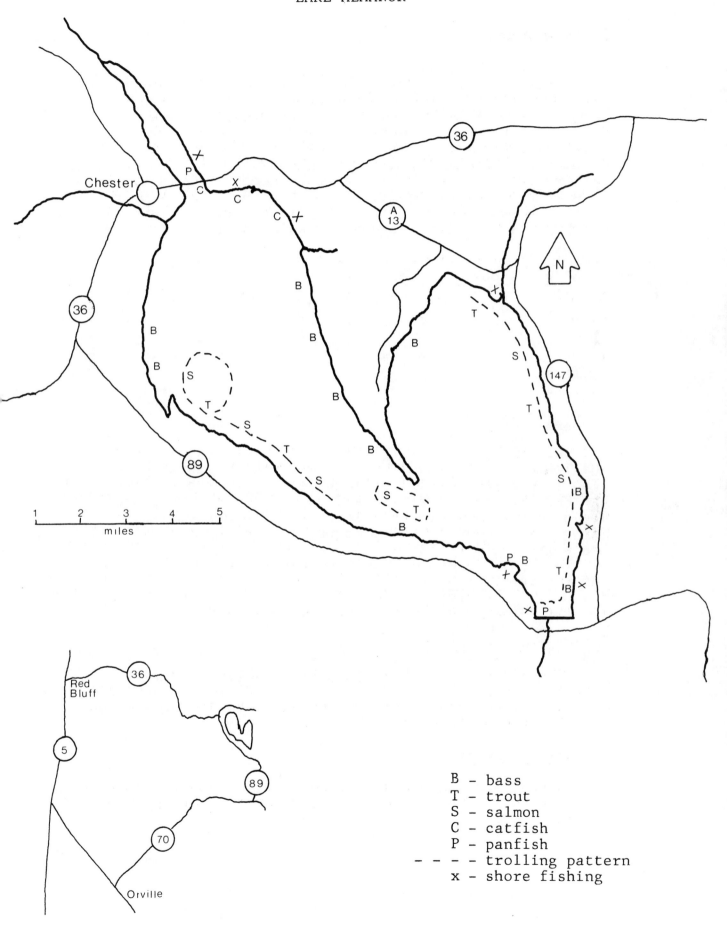

LAKE ALMANOR

B – bass
T – trout
S – salmon
C – catfish
P – panfish
– – – – trolling pattern
x – shore fishing

Lake Amador

Lake Amador is known for its trophy black bass. A record fish, which was caught at the inlet to the Jackson Arm, weighed in at 15 lbs. 9 oz. Bass catches are not only large, but they are plentiful. Trout fishing is excellent. Total trout plants are in the 60-70,000 per year range. Cat-fishing and panfishing are also good. Amador is a dedicated fishing lake. No water skiing or speedboating is allowed. This lake has about 15 miles of shoreline. It is open February through Thanksgiving. Facilities include launch ramps campgrounds, stores, restaurant, swimming pond and water slide.

Fishing Seasons (+=good, −=fair)

Species	J	F	M	A	M	J	J	A	S	O	N	D
Bass		−	+	+	−	−	−	−	−	−		
Trout	+	+	+	+	−							
Catfish			−	−	−	+	+	−	−	−		
Panfish	+	+	+	−	−	−	−	−	−			

Fishing Tips

Night fishing during full moons, for bass is good in shallow water during July and August. Use Plastic worms. Also good night fishing in lighted campgrounds for trout. Use Marshmallows. Catfish are also good in campgrounds. Use nightcrawlers, chicken livers, or anchovies. Jigs and minnows are good for crappies up to 3 pounds. Redworms and mealworms work for bluegills.

Information/Bait/Tackle

Lake Amador Resort, 7500 Lake Amador Dr., Ione, CA
(209)274-2625

Marinas and Launch Ramps	Launching Lanes	Dockage	Fuel	Boat Rental
Lake Amador Resort	6	yes	yes	yes

LAKE AMADOR

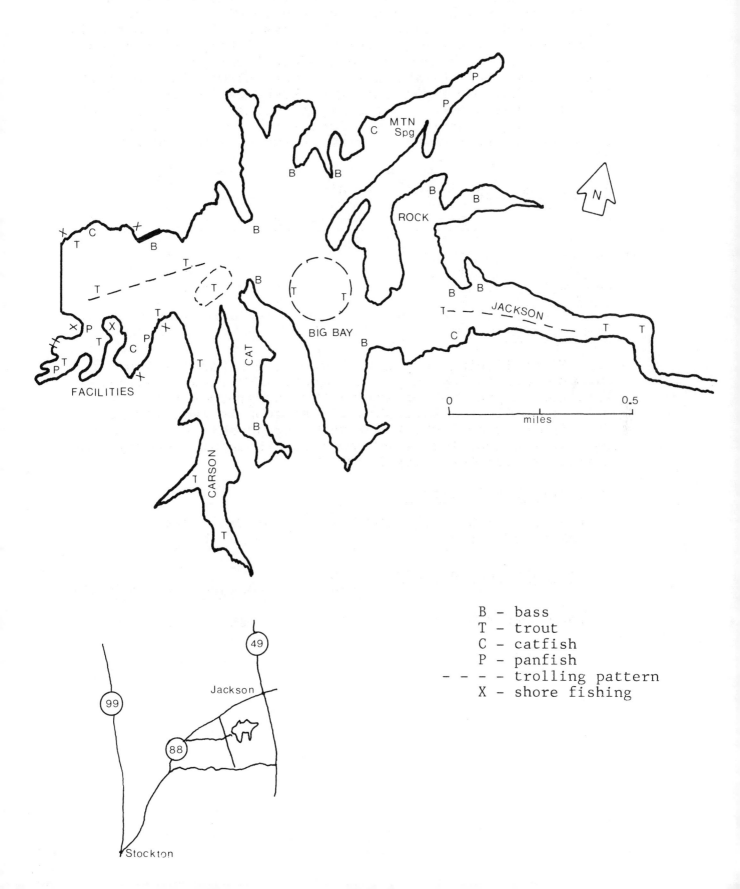

B – bass
T – trout
C – catfish
P – panfish
- - - - trolling pattern
X – shore fishing

Anderson Lake

Anderson Lake is one of a pair of lakes, the other is Coyote(just down the road), that offer good fishing within easy reach of South Bay residents. Anderson is primarily a bass, crappie and bluegill lake. Trout plants are concentrated in Coyote. Facilities at Anderson include a full service marina(Holliday Marina), 2 launch ramps and picnicing. Camping and night boating are not permitted. The lake is about 7 miles long.

Fishing Seasons (+=good, -=fair)

Species	J	F	M	A	M	J	J	A	S	O	N	D
Bass		-	-	+	+	+	-	-	-	-	-	
Catfish			-	-	-	+	+	+	-	-	-	
Panfish			-	-	-	-	-	-	-	-	-	

Fishing Tips

Bass fishing is best near the rocky points by the dam, in the coves on the north shore of the lake and in the narrows at each end of the lake. Catfish are good at the E. Dunne Avenue bridge, near the marina and at the dam. Clams, anchovies and chicken livers work good for catfish. Bass are deep in summer, from 35-50 feet. One good way to get down to bass at these depths is to vertical jig a spoon. Drop it straight down to the bottom and then lift is up a few feet and let it flutter down. Bass strike on the initial drop and on the flutter drop.

Information/Bait/Tackle

Holliday Marina, Holliday Drive, Morgan Hill, CA.
(408)779-4895

Marinas and Launch Ramps	Launching Lanes	Dockage	Fuel	Boat Rental
Holliday Marina	4	yes	yes	yes
Dam Area Launch Ramp	4	yes	no	no

ANDERSON LAKE

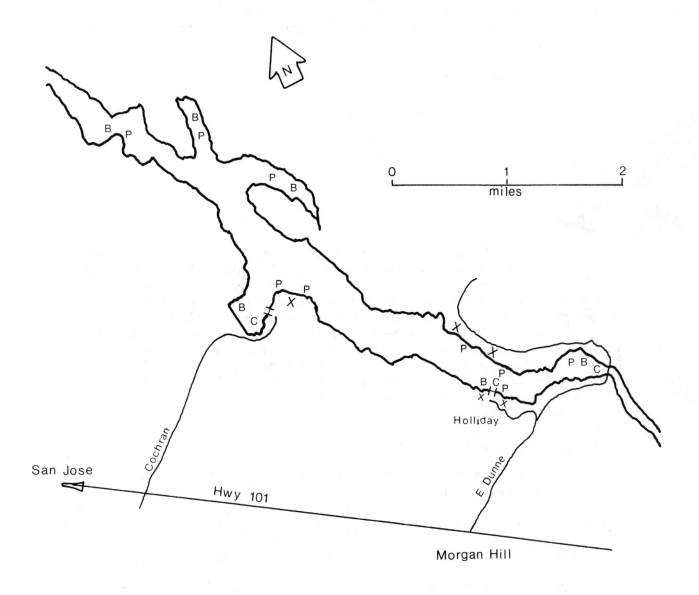

B - bass
C - catfish
P - panfish
ⲙ - launch ramp
X - shore fishing

Lake Berryessa

Berryessa is an excellent fishing lake offering most varieties of fresh water fish. It is a big lake(25 miles long) with 165 miles of shoreline. Surface water temperature of the lake is in the 70's in the summer, so successful anglers "go deep" during these months. Lake Berryessa has abundant facilities, including resorts, campgrounds, full service marinas and launchramps. It is open all year around.

Fishing Seasons (+=good, -=fair)

Species	J	F	M	A	M	J	J	A	S	O	N	D
Trout	+	+	+	+	-	-	-	-	-	-	+	+
Salmon	+	+	+	+	-	-	-	-	-	-	+	+
Bass			-	+	+	-	-	-	-	+	+	
Catfish			-	-	-	-	-	-	-	-	-	
Panfish			-	-	-	-	-	-	-	-	-	

Fishing Tips

Rainbow Trout and King Salmon are taken when the lake is stratified by deep(30-80 ft.) trolling Kastmasters, Triple Teasers, Mr. Champs and other metal lures that imitate the shad bait fish. Use a flasher. Topline or surface trolling is very productive for these same fish in cooler months, using nightcrawlers or minnows. Trolling is most successful in the southern portion of the lake, in the narrows all the way to the dam. Catfish can be found in the warm, shallow coves using clams, chicken livers, anchovies, etc. Bass fishing is good off rocky points and in deep coves. Crappies take mini-jigs and minnows. Bluegill fishing is good with redworms and mealworms. Still fishing, from shore or boat, is very productive for Trout in the cooler months.

Information/Bait/Tackle

There are numerous sources of fishing information, and bait and tackle shops at Lake Berryessa. Many of the resorts and marinas, as well as several sporting goods stores are anxious to provide information and supplies.

Marinas and Launch Ramps

There are a number of full service marinas at Lake Berryessa, each with launch ramps, docks, fuel and boat rental All are located along the southwest shore of the lake.

LAKE BERRYESSA

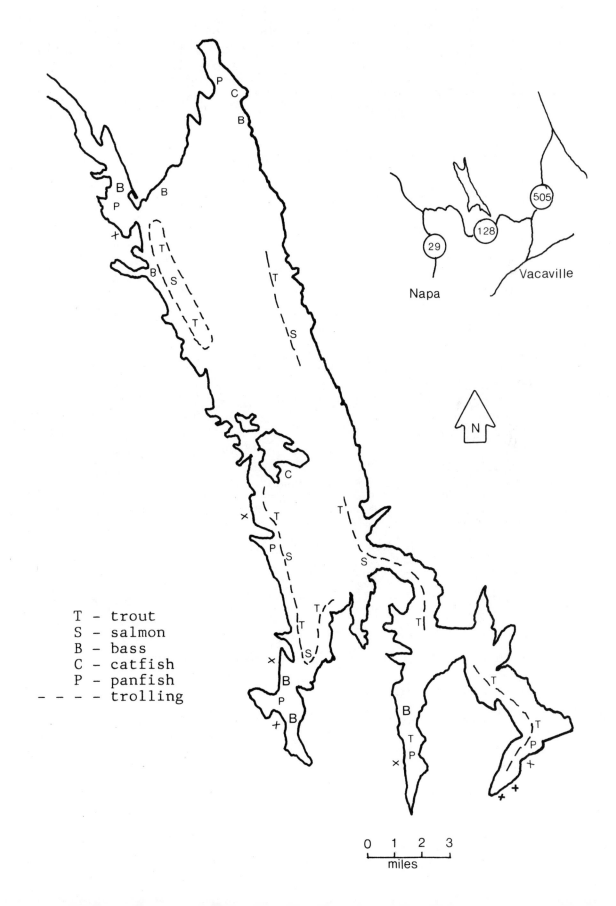

T – trout
S – salmon
B – bass
C – catfish
P – panfish
- - - - trolling

Napa

Vacaville

29

128

505

N

0 1 2 3
miles

Camanche Lake

Camanche is a fine motherlode fishing lake. Offerings
include trout(rainbow and Eagle Lake), bass(including Florida
and Alabama Spotted), king salmon, catfish(channel and white)
and panfish. Camanche is a sizeable lake(53 miles of shoreline) and has camping, recreation and launching facilities
on both the south shore and north shore. It is open all year.
Facilities include campground, swimming, waterslide, stable,
and store.

Fishing Seasons   (+=good, -=fair)

Species	J	F	M	A	M	J	J	A	S	O	N	D
Trout	+	+	+	+	-	-	-	-	-	-	+	+
Salmon	+	+	+	+	-	-	-	-	-	-	+	+
Bass			-	+	+	-	-	-	-	+	+	
Catfish		-	+	+	+	+	-	-	-	+	+	
Panfish		-	-	-	-	-	-	-	-	-	-	

Fishing Tips

Trout fishing can be productive all year at Camanche.
Trout are down 12-15 feet in cooler months and as much as
30-50 feet in warm months. Look for them always at 55° water
temperature. The night bite for trout is often good. Some
bass can be caught in shallow water(less than 10 feet) during
spring, summer and fall. Lead head jigs, spinner baits, and
plastic worms are the most productive. Camanche has a healthy
population of catfish. Chicken livers is a popular bait,
especially for boat fishermen.

Information/Bait/Tackle

South Camanche Shore, P.O. Box 92, Wallace, CA 95254
    (209)763-5178

North Camanche Shore, 2000 Jackson Valley-Camanche Rd.,
    (209)763-5151   Ione, CA 95640

Marinas and Launch Ramps	Launching Lanes	Dockage	Fuel	Boat Rental
South Shore	7	yes	yes	yes
North Shore	5	yes	yes	yes

CAMANCHE LAKE

T – trout
S – salmon
B – bass
C – catfish
P – panfish
⊥ – launch ramp
– – – – trolling pattern
x – shore fishing

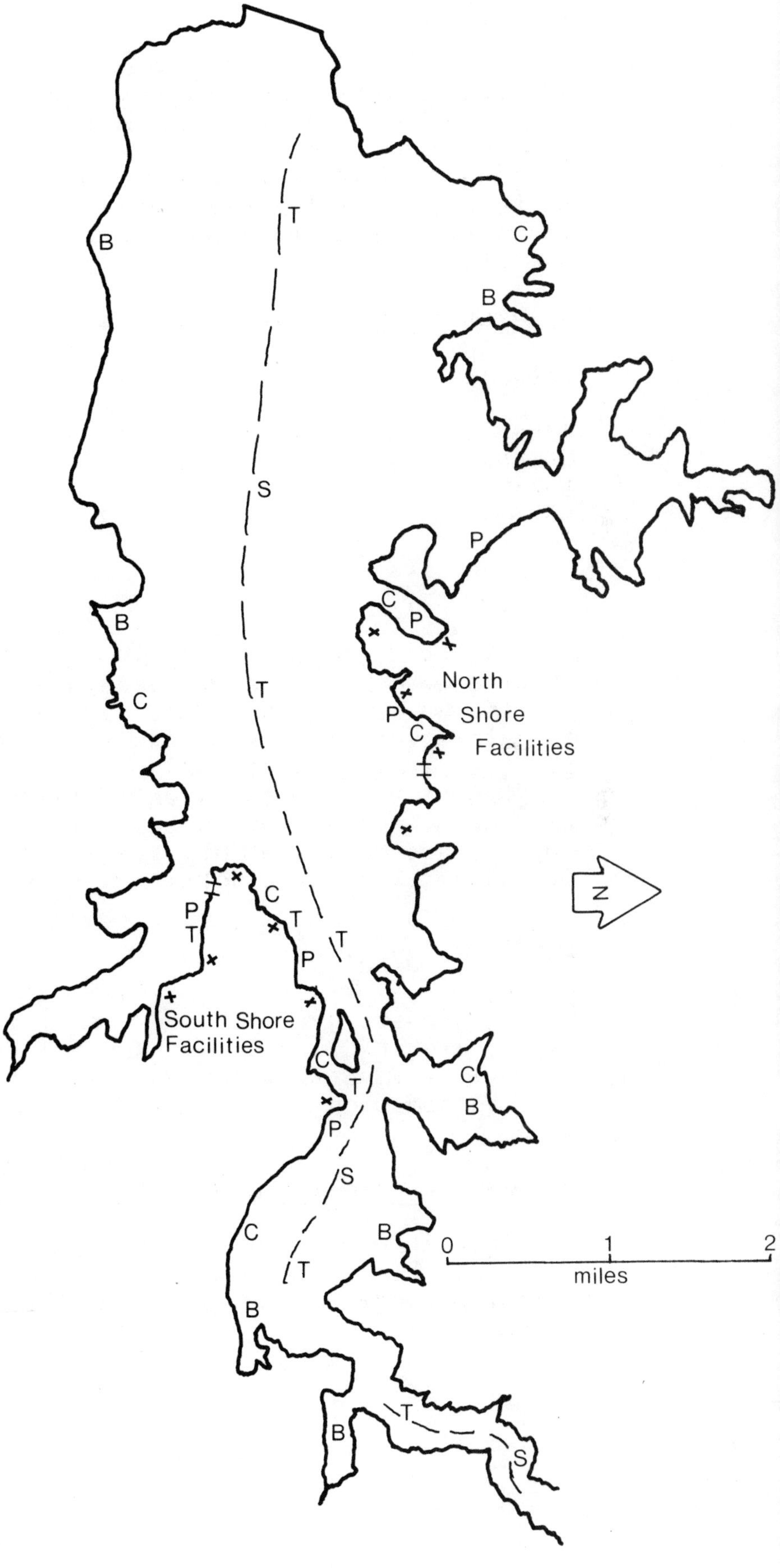

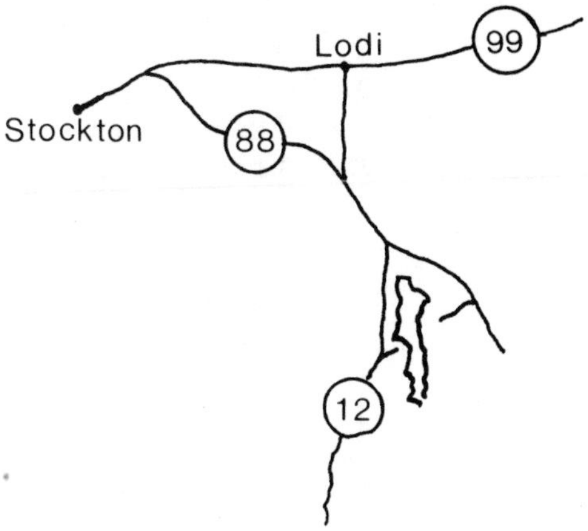

B

C

B

P

C   P

North
Shore
Facilities

P

C

T

S

T

P

T

C   T

P   T

T

P

x

South Shore
Facilities

C

C

T

B

P

S

C

B

B

T

Lodi   99

Stockton   88

12

0   1   2

miles

B

T

S

N

Clear Lake

Clear Lake is an excellent "warm water" fishing lake, offering great bass fishing as well as catfishing and pan-fishing. This is the largest natural lake entirely within the state of California. It is about 20 miles long and has about 100 miles of shoreline. Clear Lake has numerous facilities that include resorts, state parks, full service marinas and launch ramps. These are distributed all around the lake.

Fishing Seasons (+=good, -=fair)

Species	J	F	M	A	M	J	J	A	S	O	N	D
Bass			+	+	+	-	-	-	-	+	+	
Catfish	-	-	-	-	+	+	+	+	-	-		
Panfish	-	-	-	-	-	-	-	-	-	-		

Fishing Tips

Clear Lake bills itself as the "Bass Capitol of the West" and is the host of many black bass tournaments. Tule beds provide cover for the bass and are productive fishing locales. Plastic worms, spinner baits and Pig-N-Jigs are productive offerings for bass. Catfishing is very good in Clear Lake. Catfish ranging from 10-20 pounds are not uncommon. The best catfish bite is in the evening from about 9pm to 1 in the morning. Another good bite is from 4am to 7am. The largest catfish are caught at night. Waxworms are good offerings for bluegill at boat docks and grassy coves.

Information/Bait/Tackle

There are numerous sources of fishing information, bait and tackle at Clear Lake. Many of the resorts and marinas, as well as several sporting goods stores are anxious to provide information and supplies.

Marinas and Launch Ramps

There are numerous full service marinas on Clear Lake, each with launch ramps, docks, fuel and boat rental. Free launch ramps are located in Lakeport, Nice, Lucerne, Clearlake and Soda Bay.

CLEAR LAKE

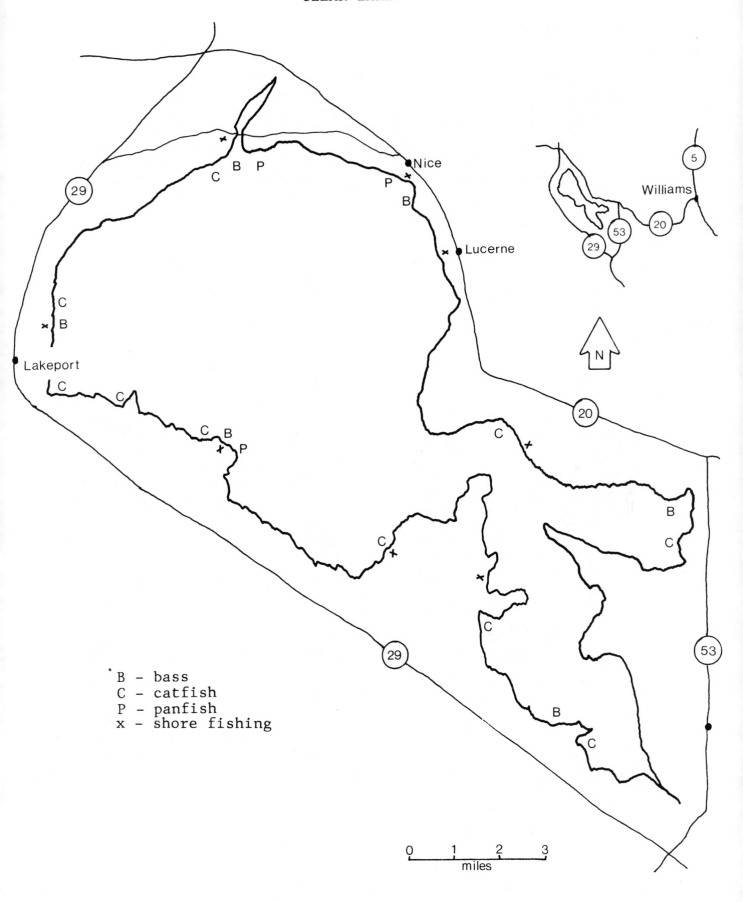

B – bass
C – catfish
P – panfish
x – shore fishing

Don Pedro Lake

Don Pedro is an excellent fishing lake, offering a wide variety including rainbow and Eagle Lake trout, silver and king salmon, largemouth bass, catfish, crappies and blue-gills. It is a large lake, 26 miles long with 160 miles of shoreline. Don Pedro has three major facilities. Each has camping and launching facilities. Trout range in size up to 6 pounds. Salmon are generally in the 2 to 4 pound range. Typical bass are 1½ pounds, but range up to 8-10 pounds. The lake has recently been planted with the fast growing Florida black bass. Night fishing is allowed.

Fishing Seasons (+=good, -=fair)

Species	J	F	M	A	M	J	J	A	S	O	N	D
Trout	+	+	+	+	-	-	-	-	-	-	+	+
Salmon	+	+	+	+	-	-	-	-	-	-	+	+
Bass			-	+	+	-	-	-	-	+	+	-
Catfish			-	-	-	-	-	-	-	-	-	
Panfish		+	+	+	-	-	-	-	-	-	+	

Fishing Tips

Trolling is the most productive method of catching trout and salmon. Silver lures, including Needlefish, Kastmasters, Phoebes, Triple Teasers and Z-Rays, are all winners. Casting can also be productive in the spring. Still fishing, using a sliding sinker rig and salmon egg-marshmallow combination bait, works good for trout and salmon. Try near, or across from Fleming Meadows Marina. Spinnerbaits and plastic worms work good for bass. Mini-jigs produce for crappies. Redworms and mealworms for bluegills.

Information/Bait/Tackle

Lake Don Pedro Marina, Star Route, Box 81, LaGrange, CA.
   (209)852-2369   95329

Davis Bait & Tackle
   (209)634-0311

Marinas and Launch Ramps	Launching Lanes	Dockage	Fuel	Boat Rental
Lake Don Pedro Marina	12	yes	yes	yes

DON PEDRO LAKE

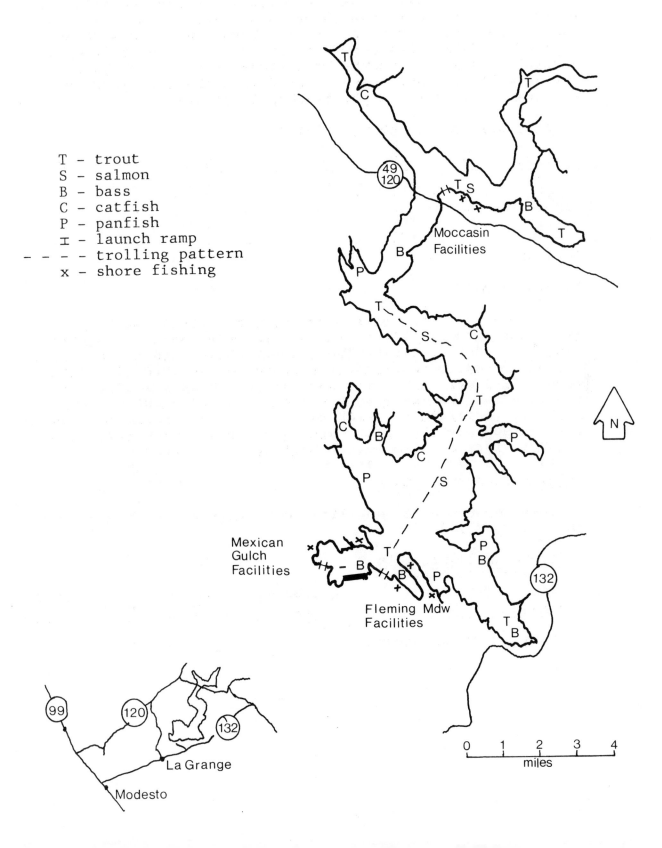

T - trout
S - salmon
B - bass
C - catfish
P - panfish
⊥ - launch ramp
- - - - trolling pattern
x - shore fishing

Moccasin
Facilities

Mexican
Gulch
Facilities

Fleming Mdw
Facilities

N

99   120   132

La Grange

Modesto

0   1   2   3   4
miles

Eagle Lake

Eagle Lake is the home of the famous Eagle Lake rainbow trout. Eagle Lake trout are said by many to fight like steelhead and taste like coho salmon. Eagle Lake is a large (16 miles long), natural body of water located at high altitude(5100 feet) in the northern Sierras. Its waters are so alkaline that only the Eagle Lake trout and a small minnow called the tui chub can survive there. Eagle Lake trout are good-sized fish. The lake record is almost 11 pounds, 4-6 pounders are frequently caught and 1-2 pound fish are common. Facilities include a full service marina, camping and several resorts.

Fishing Seasons (+=good, -=fair)

Species	J	F	M	A	M	J	J	A	S	O	N	D
Eagle Lake Trout	——————closed———————					+	+	+	+	+	+	

Fishing Tips

As is true in many trout lakes, trolling is the surest way to catch Eagle Lake trout. Offerings(behind flashers) include Speedy Shiners, Needlefish, Z-Rays, Triple Teasers, Kastmasters and Rapalas. Good shore fishing for Eagle rainbow exists. Best locations include Wildcat Point on the west side, Pelican Point(at narrow lake section) and Eagle's Nest(directly in front of the cabins on the east side). Nightcrawlers are the most productive still fishing bait. Inflate them and use a sliding sinker rig. In the fall, many boat anglers still fish, using nightcrawlers, over the springs. Look for the boats, that's where the springs are. One last hint. Fish early in the a.m., the bite usually ends by 8 or 9 a.m.

Information/Bait/Tackle

Eagle Lake Marina, Box 128, Dept. FS, Susanville, CA. 96130

Marinas and Launch Ramps	Launching Lanes	Dockage	Fuel	Boat Rental
Eagle Lake Marina	3	yes	yes	yes

EAGLE LAKE

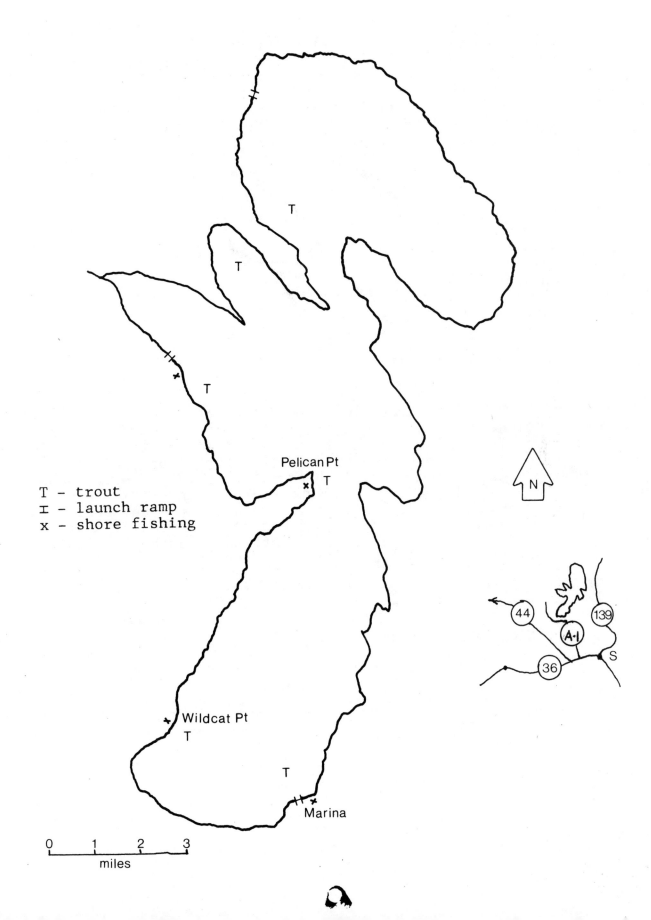

T - trout
ɪ - launch ramp
x - shore fishing

Pelican Pt

Wildcat Pt

Marina

0   1   2   3
miles

Lake Nacimiento

Lake Nacimiento, which is just south of San Antonio Lake, provides one of the few white bass fisheries in Northern California. In addition to the excellent white bass fishing, there is also black bass, crappies, catfish and carp in Lake Nacimiento. White bass are prolific and can damage trout and striped bass fisheries. Therefore, the limit at Nacimiento for white bass has been removed but no live white bass may be in possession. No one wants white bass to take over other lakes. Facilities at Nacimiento include store, campground and launch ramp. The lake has 165 miles of shoreline.

Fishing Seasons   (+=good, -=fair)

Species	J	F	M	A	M	J	J	A	S	O	N	D
Wh. Bass			+	+	+	+						
Bass		−	+	+	−	−	−	−	−			
Catfish			−	−	−	+	+	+	+	−		
Panfish			−	−	−	−	−	−	−	−		

Fishing Tips

There are several ways to catch white bass. Trolling small Rooster Tails, Kastmasters, Hopkins Spoons are good bets. Casting these same offerings into boiling schools of shad is also very productive. Care should be taken to approach the boil gently so as not to drive down the school. Spoons should be in the 1/4 to 3/8 oz. range. White bass average 2-3 pounds. Bluegills are available throughout the lake, especially at drop-offs and coves. Mealworms are suggested. Summers are good for catfish on anchovies and chicken livers. Spring is a good time for bowfishing for carp.

Information/Bait/Tackle

Nacimiento Resort, Bradley, CA. 93426
(805)228-3256

Marinas and Launch Ramps	Launching Lanes	Dockage	Fuel	Boat Rental
Nacimiento Resort	3	yes	yes	yes

LAKE NACIMIENTO

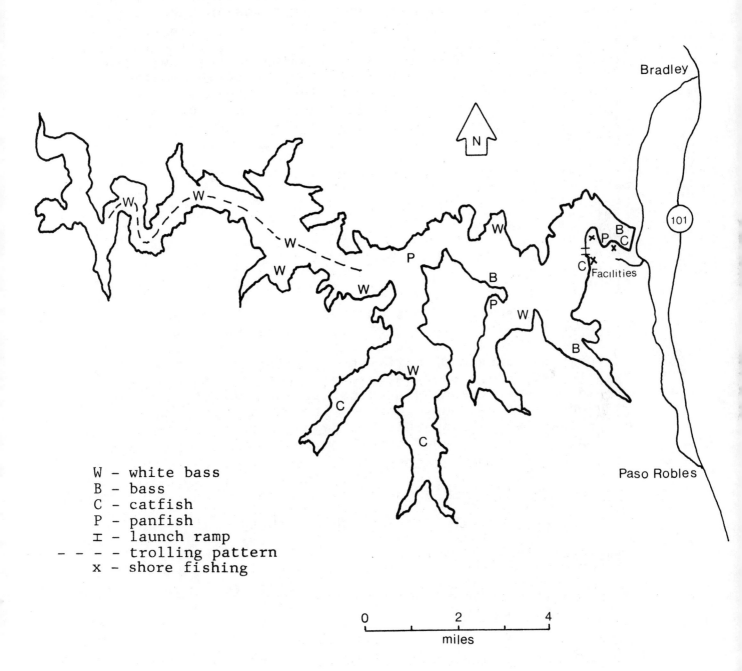

W – white bass
B – bass
C – catfish
P – panfish
⌐ – launch ramp
– – – – trolling pattern
x – shore fishing

New Hogan Lake

New Hogan is an excellent fishing lake, offering trout, bass, catfish and panfish. Also, its striped bass fishing is developing rapidly, with average catches in the 8-10 pound range. The record striper is 18 pounds. A coho salmon fishery is also coming on. Facilities at New Hogan include camping, swimming, marina, store, and launch ramps. The lake has 50 miles of shoreline. There is also a boat-in camping area.

Fishing Seasons   (+=good, -=fair)

Species	J	F	M	A	M	J	J	A	S	O	N	D
Trout	-	+	+	+	+	-	-	-	-	-	-	-
Bass		-	+	+	+	-	-	-	-	-		
Str. Bass		-	-	-	-	-	-	+	+	+		
Catfish		-	-	-	-	+	+	+	-			
Panfish		-	-	-	-	-	-	-	-			

Fishing Tips

Trout fishing is best in the narrows in the northeast section of the lake, both from shore and by boat. Trollers in the narrows for trout also pick up salmon. Stripers are caught primarily by trolling silver Kastmasters(1-2oz.) and broken back Rebel lures. Depth of troll depends on the season. Stripers are also caught by plugging when shad boil up. Chicken livers, anchovies and clams are productive catfish baits. Crappie fishing is not consistant, but can be good from time to time.

Information/Bait/Tackle

New Hogan Marina, 1955 New Hogan Parkway, Valley Springs, (209)772-1462
CA.

Marinas and Launch Ramps	Launching Lanes	Dockage	Fuel	Boat Rental
New Hogan Marina	13	yes	yes	yes

NEW HOGAN LAKE

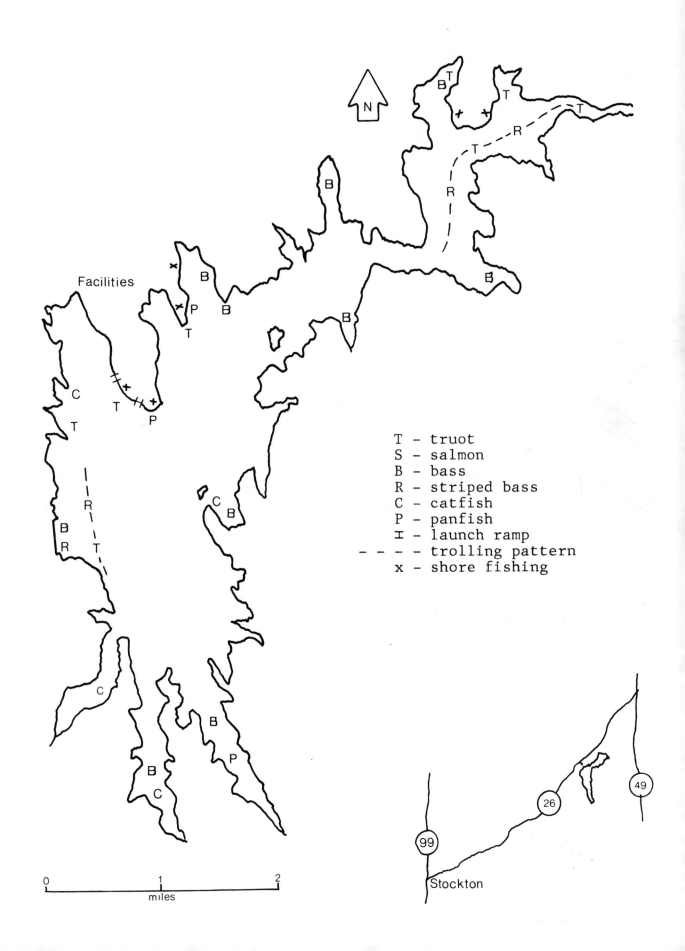

T – truot
S – salmon
B – bass
R – striped bass
C – catfish
P – panfish
I – launch ramp
- - - - trolling pattern
x – shore fishing

Facilities

Stockton

99   26   49

0   1   2
miles

New Melones Lake

New Melones reservoir is a new reservoir that offers excellent fishing. However, shore facilities such as camping, are still under development. Species include trout(rainbow and brown), king salmon, bass(both largemouth and smallmouth), catfish and panfish. This is a large lake(about 8 miles across) that extends up the Stanislaus River canyon over 10 miles. Campsites are available at Glory Hole Recreation Area and picnic facilities are available at Tuttletown. Night fishing is permitted, as is waterskiing and swimming.

Fishing Seasons   (+=good, -=fair)

Species	J	F	M	A	M	J	J	A	S	O	N	D
Trout	+	+	+	+	-	-	-	-	-	-	-	+
Salmon	+	+	+	+	-	-	-	-	-	-	-	+
Bass		-	+	+	+	-	-	-	-	-	-	
Catfish		-	-	-	-	-	-	-	-	-		
Panfish		-	-	-	-	-	-	-	-	-		

Fishing Tips

As is true in other locations, at New Melones the larger fish are usually found in deeper water. This is true for trout, salmon, bass and crappies. So, if you're trolling and catching smallish trout, drop it down 5-10 feet and you're likely to pick up some larger fish. Along the same vane, salmon trollers in the summer go down 75-100 feet, whereas trout trollers hit at 35-60 feet. Still fishing, off the dam and spillway, is often good for trout and salmon, especially during evenings and nights.

Information/Bait/Tackle

Creekside Sports, 484 E. Hwy. 4, Murphys, CA 95247
   (209)728-2166

Vern's Liquors & Sporting Goods, Hwy. 49, Angel's Camp
   (209)736-2205
Vern's   "   "   "   Hwy. 4, Murphys, CA
   (209)728-3281

Marinas and Launch Ramps	Launching Lanes	Dockage	Fuel	Boat Rental
Glory Hole Rec. Area	yes	no	no	no
Tuttletown Rec. Area	yes	no	no	no

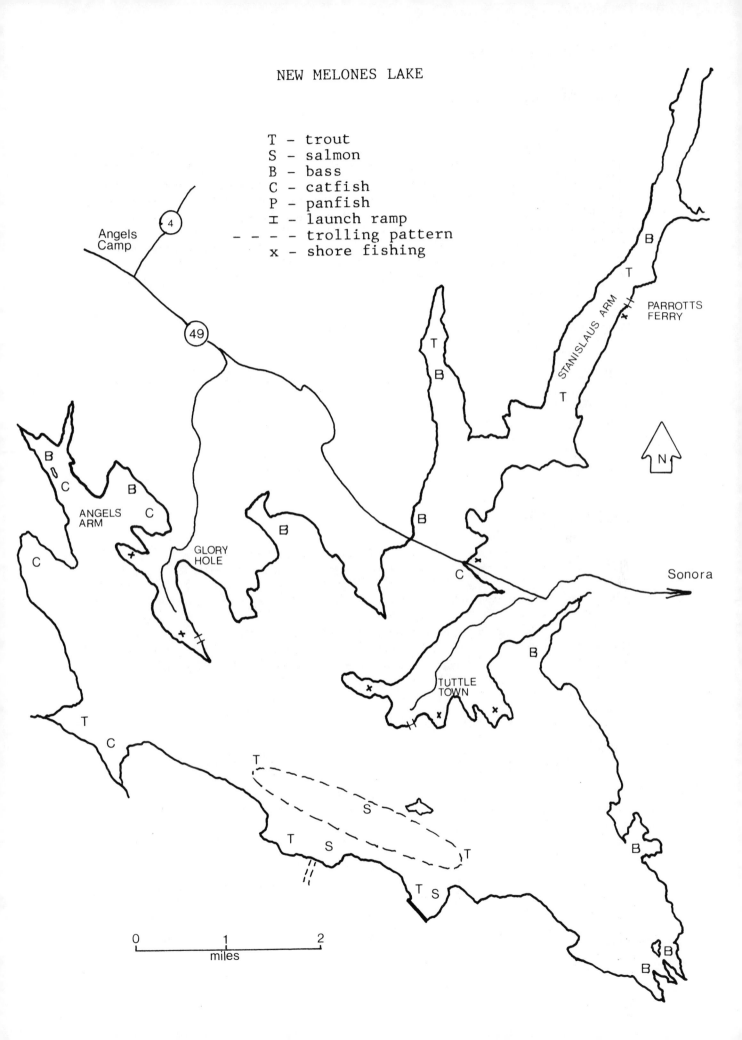

NEW MELONES LAKE

T – trout
S – salmon
B – bass
C – catfish
P – panfish
⊥ – launch ramp
– – – – trolling pattern
x – shore fishing

Lake Oroville

Lake Oroville is a very large, beautiful reservoir that offers excellent fishing. Trout, salmon, bass, catfish and panfish are all plentiful. This canyon reservoir is made up of the branches of the Feather River. Camping is concentrated at two locations at the south end of the lake with full service marinas at both the south and north end of the lake. Shore fishing is limited because of the steep shoreline and limited access opportunities. The best shore fishing is at campgrounds and marinas, and in the Diversion Pool, Thermalito Forebay and Afterbay(that surround the city of Oroville). The lake itself has 167 miles of shoreline.

Fishing Seasons   (+=good, -=fair)

Species	J	F	M	A	M	J	J	A	S	O	N	D
Trout	+	+	+	+	-	-	-	-	-	-	+	+
Salmon	+	+	+	+	-	-	-	-	-	-	+	+
Bass		-	+	+	+	-	-	-	-	+	+	
Catfish					-	-	-	-	-			
Panfish		-	-	-	-	-	-	-	-	-	-	

Fishing Tips

As a maturing canyon lake, Oroville is probably better for smallmouth then for largemouth bass. Oroville is actually 3 separate lakes, from a fishing point of view. The southern forks warm up first in the spring, so bassing turns on first there. The main body warms next with the north fork warming last. Besides water temperature, keep an eye on your fish locator for the threadfin shad. If they're near the surface, that's where you'll find the bass and trout. If they're down, the gamefish will also be down. Since Oroville is a very deep(over 500 feet) lake, the fish can go very deep to find food and comfortable water temperatures.

Information/Bait/Tackle

Bidwell Canyon Marina, Oroville-Quincy Road, Oroville, CA.
  (916)589-3165
Limesaddle Marine, P.O. Box 1088, Paradise, CA 95969
  (916)534-6950
Huntington's Sportsman's Store, 601 Oro Dam Blvd., Oroville,
  (916)534-8000   CA 95965

Marinas and Launch Ramps	Launching Lanes	Dockage	Fuel	Boat Rental
Bidwell Canyon Marina	7	yes	yes	yes
Loafer Creek Campground	7	no	no	no
Limesaddle Marina	5	yes	yes	yes
Spillway Boat Ramp	13	no	no	no

LAKE OROVILLE

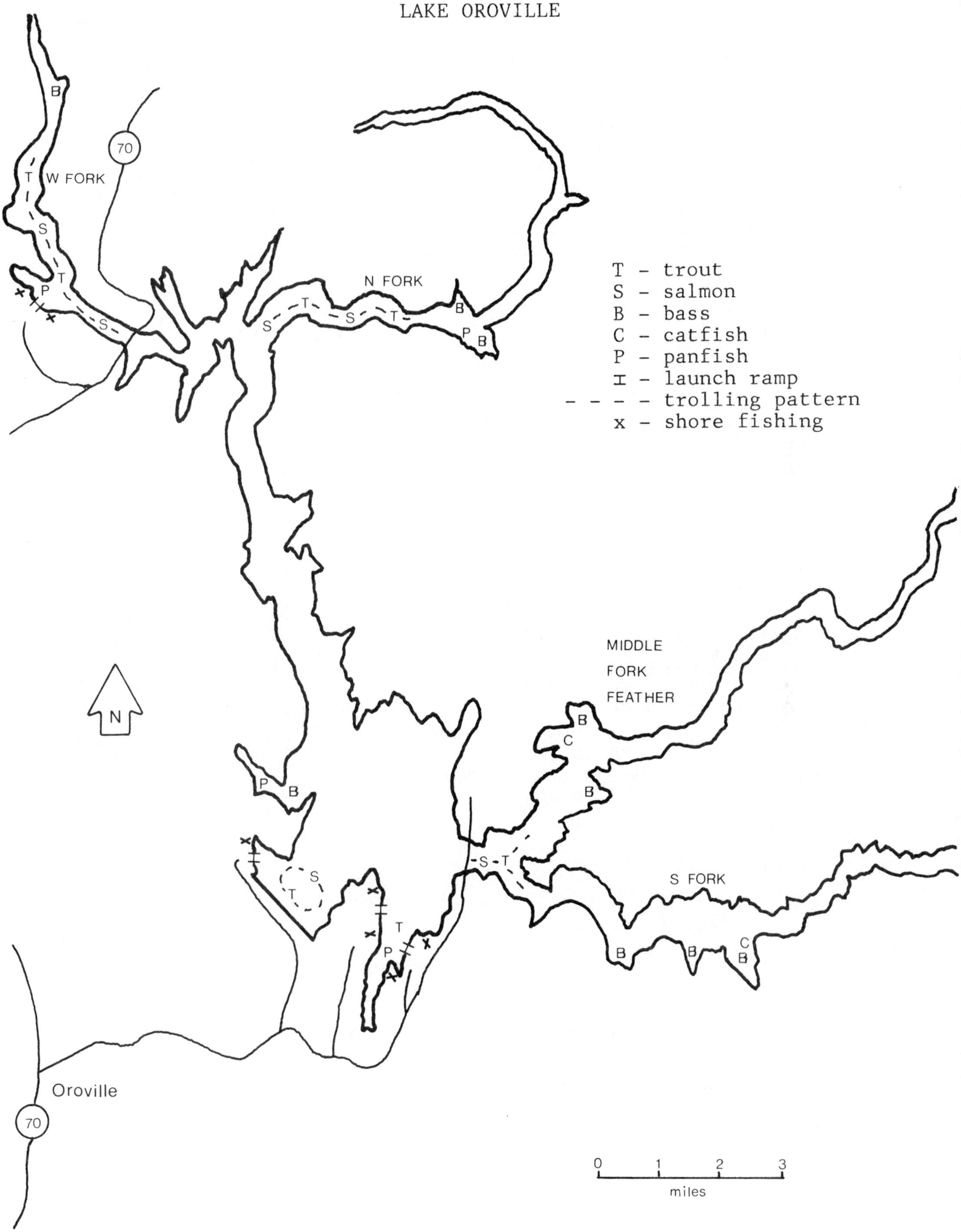

T – trout
S – salmon
B – bass
C – catfish
P – panfish
⊥ – launch ramp
– – – – trolling pattern
x – shore fishing

W FORK

N FORK

MIDDLE
FORK
FEATHER

S FORK

N

Oroville

70

70

0   1   2   3
miles

Pardee Lake

Pardee offers well-rounded fishing, but is best known for excellent trout. Trout in the 3-4 pound class are not uncommon. It is a dedicated fishing lake. No waterskiing is allowed. The waters of Pardee are clean and clear. It was built in the 1920's as an East Bay Municipal Utility District reservoir. Facilities include campground, restaurant, store, launch ramp and two swimming pools. Pardee has about 37 miles of shoreline.

Fishing Seasons   (+=good, -=fair)

Species	J	F	M	A	M	J	J	A	S	O	N	D
Trout		+	+	+	+	+	+	+	-	-		
Kokanee	-	-	+	+	+	+	-	-	-			
Bass	-	-	+	+	-	-	-	-	-			
Catfish		-	-	-	+	+	+	-	-			
Panfish		-	-	-	-	-	-	-	-			

Fishing Tips

Trout fishing is good both from shore and boat. Shore anglers use nightcrawlers(inflated) or salmon eggs(floated with marshmallows), or cast Kastmasters, Phoebes and Krocodiles. Boat trollers hit with Needlefish, Kokanee King, etc., near the surface in spring and down deeper as surface temperatures rise. Kokanee are caught by trout trollers. They school, so repeat a productive troll. Bluegills and perch hit redworms hung from bobbers. Bass fishing is best in coves and points on channel arms.

Information/Bait/Tackle

Pardee Lake Resort, 4900 Stoney Creek Rd., Ione, CA.
    (209)772-1472   95640

Marinas and Launch Ramps	Launching Lanes	Dockage	Fuel	Boat Rental
Pardee Lake Resort	10	yes	yes	yes

PARDEE LAKE

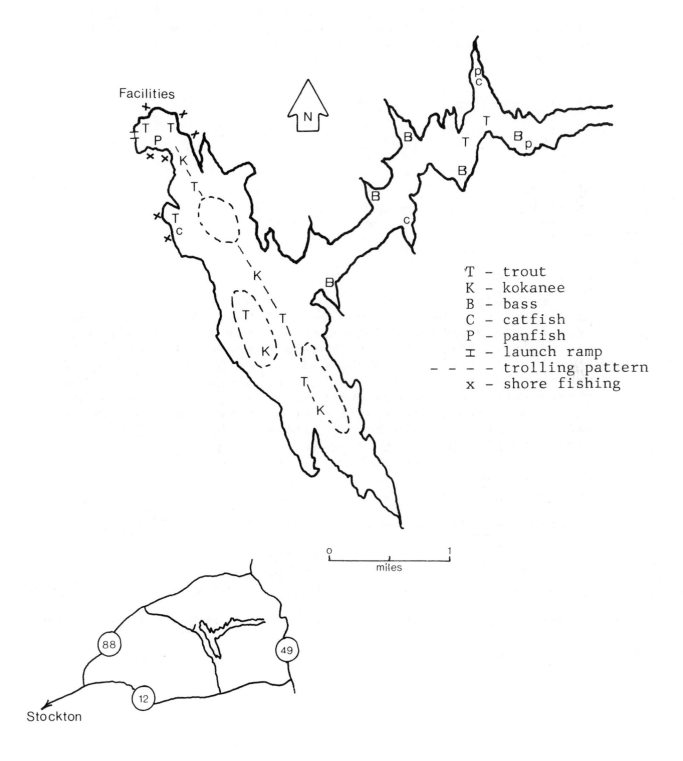

T - trout
K - kokanee
B - bass
C - catfish
P - panfish
⊥ - launch ramp
- - - - trolling pattern
x - shore fishing

Facilities

N

miles

88   49

12

Stockton

San Antonio Lake

San Antonio provides the traditional fishing fare of trout, black bass, catfish and panfish, but, in addition, offers an excellent striped bass fishery. The average striper caught is in the 15 pound range! This reservoir, about 16 miles long, is operated by the Monterey County Parks and Recreation Department. Facilities include camping, restaurant, store, launch ramps and swimming.

Fishing Seasons   (+=good, -=fair)

Species	J	F	M	A	M	J	J	A	S	O	N	D
Trout	+	+	+	-	-	-	-	-	-	-	+	+
Bass			-	-	+	+	-	-	-	-		
Str. Bass			-	-	-	+	+	+	-	-		
Catfish			-	-	-	-	+	+	+	-		
Panfish			-	-	-	-	-	-	-	-		

Fishing Tips

One rule that seems to apply to all the fisheries in San Antonio is that the bite is best near shore early in the day and then moves into deeper water later in the day. So, if the action slows, move into deeper water rather than quit. Most trout are in the ½-1 pound range and hit on Kastmasters, Rooster Tails, or salmon egg-marshmallow combinations. Striped bass are mostly caught trolling Hopkins Spoons are a favorite trolling lure at San Antonio. Troll near the surface near shore in the mornings. Then move deeper and farther from shore later in the day. Harris Creek is one of the most productive spots on the lake for largemouth bass and crappies.

Information/Bait/Tackle

Lake San Antonio, Bradley CA. 93426
   (805)472-2311

Marinas and Launch Ramps	Launching Lanes	Dockage	Fuel	Boat Rental
Lake San Antonio	3	yes	yes	yes

SAN ANTONIO LAKE

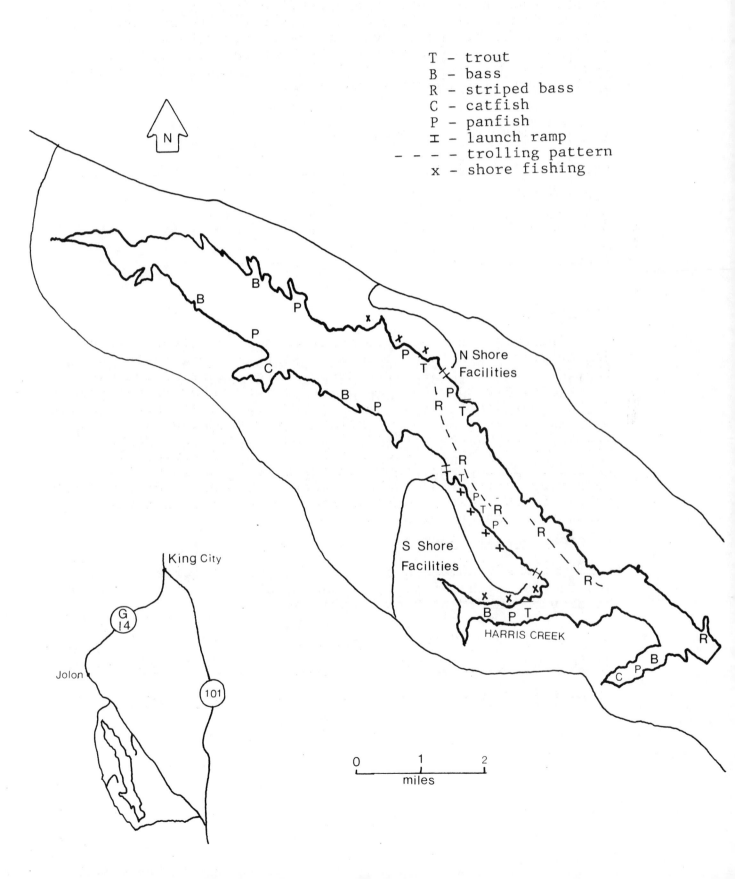

T – trout
B – bass
R – striped bass
C – catfish
P – panfish
I – launch ramp
- - - - trolling pattern
x – shore fishing

N

B
B
P
P
C
B P
x
x
x
P
P T
N Shore
Facilities
R
P
T
R
T
+
P
+ T R
+ P
R
+
R
S Shore
Facilities
x
x
x
B P T
HARRIS CREEK
R
C P B

King City
G 14
Jolon
101

0   1   2
miles

San Luis Reservoir

San Luis Reservoir and the adjoining O'Neill Forebay offer very good fishing, especially for striped bass. Water (and small fingerling and fry stripers) are pumped into the resevoir from the Sacramento, San Joaquin and the Delta, primarily during the winter and spring. This pumping process and numerous bait fish, produces an abundant supply of striper, most in the 3-8 pound range. But fish over 25 pounds are caught on occasion. Camping and launching facilities are available. But, note that strong winds are common on the reservoir itself. San Luis has 65 miles of shoreline.

Fishing Seasons   (+=good, -=fair)

Species	J	F	M	A	M	J	J	A	S	O	N	D
Striper		−	+	+	+	−			−	+	−	
Catfish		−	−	−	+	+	+	−	−			

Fishing Tips

Stripers feed on threadfin shad. When these bait fish school on the surface, watch for bird action to pinpoint the striper schools feeding on the shad. A popular way to take striper at San Luis is casting from a boat. About ½ oz. Kastmasters, Krocodiles and Hair-raisers are productive. Early morning and late evening are the best times. Shore fishing for stripers, using pileworms and anchovies, is popular at the Basalt Area and in the Forebay. Striper limit is 5 fish of any size. Stripers also go for trolled Rebels, Kastmasters, etc,.

Information/Bait/Tackle

There are numerous sources of fishing information, bait and tackle in the vicinity of San Luis. They are all anxious to provide information and supplies.

Marinas and Launch Ramps	Launching Lanes	Dockage	Fuel	Boat Rental
San Luis Reservoir	2	no	no	no
O'Neill Forebay	2	no	no	no

SAN LOUIS RESERVOIR

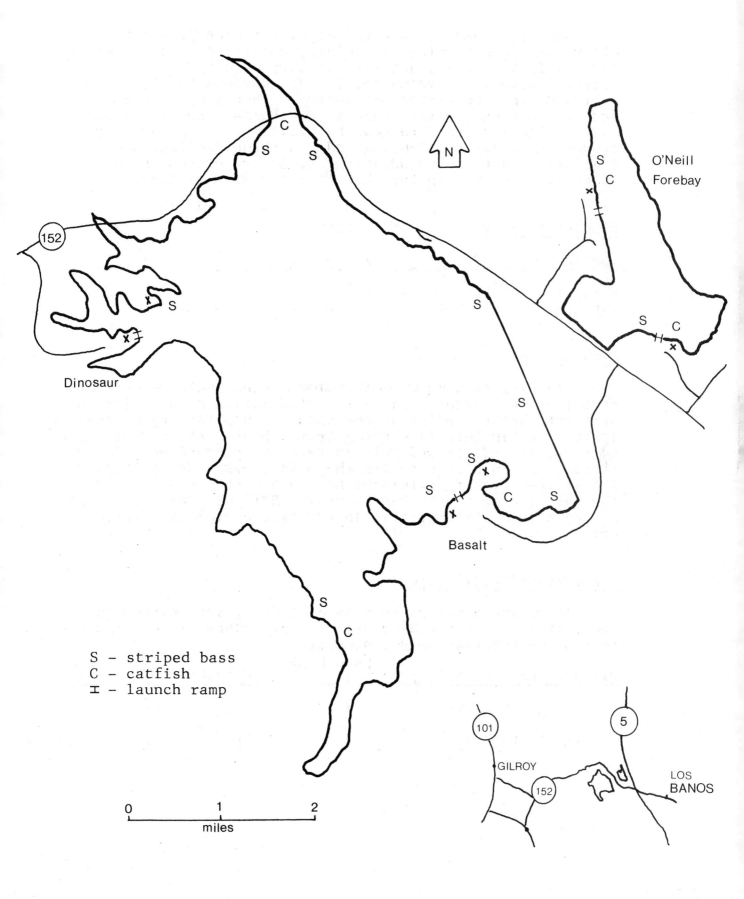

S - striped bass
C - catfish
ɪ - launch ramp

O'Neill
Forebay

Dinosaur

Basalt

GILROY

LOS
BANOS

0   1   2
miles

San Pablo Reservoir

Excellent fishing is available at this day-use reservoir located just east of the San Francisco Bay near Berkeley. San Pablo Reservoir is a narrow reservoir about 4 miles long. The lakes record rainbow is 14½ pounds, and many are caught in the 3-6 pound range. Trout plants, done weekly, average about 1 pound per fish. Anglers at San Pablo frequently average 2-3 trout per rod, from both boat and shore. The only live bait allowed at San Pablo is redworms and night-crawlers. San Pablo offers many good shore fishing locations for trout and catfish. For boaters, a topographical map showing the holes to fish, is for sale at the lake for less than $1.00. Closed from mid-November to mid-February.

Fishing Seasons   (+=good, -=fair)

Species	J	F	M	A	M	J	J	A	S	O	N	D
Trout		+	+	+	+	-	-	-	-	+	+	
Bass		+	+	+	-	-	-	-	-			
Catfish		-	-	-	-	-	-	-	-			
Panfish		-	-	-	-	-	-	-	-			

Fishing Tips

Trout shore fishing at San Pablo is best using a sliding sinker rig and salmon eggs, marshmallows, nightcrawlers and cheese. Inflating nightcrawlers or using marshmallows to float up eggs, nightcralwers or cheese(to keep bait off the bottom). Casting spinners and spoons also works from shore. Boat trout anglers troll(behind flashers) night-crawlers, Rooster Tails, Triple Teasers, Needlefish, Kast-masters and Panther Martins. Bass go for 4" plastic worms, spinnerbait and Pig-N-Jigs.

Information/Bait/Tackle

That Dam Company, 7301 San Pablo Dr., El Sobrante, CA.94803
(415)223-1661

Marinas and Launch Ramps	Launching Lanes	Dockage	Fuel	Boat Rental
That Dam Company	4	yes	yes	yes

SAN PABLO RESERVOIR

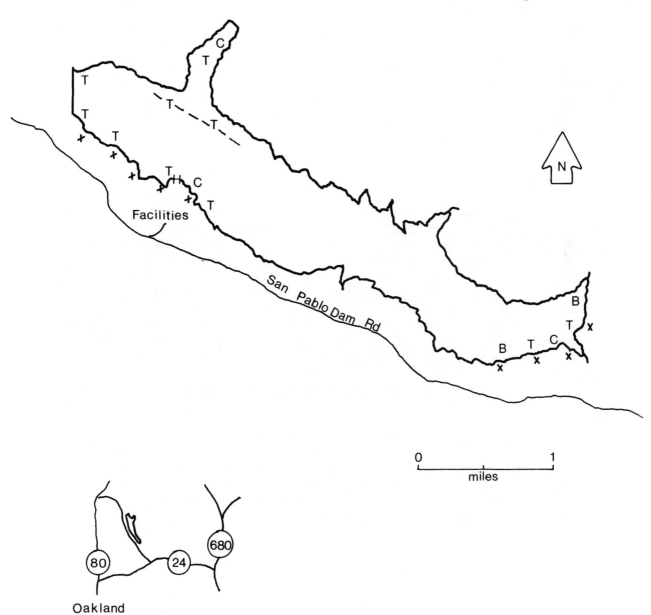

T – trout
B – bass
C – catfish
P – panfish
⌐ – launch ramp
– – – – trolling pattern
x – shore fishing

C

T

T

T

T

T

T

T

x

x

T

C

x

T

C

Facilities

San Pablo Dam Rd

N

B

T

x

B

T

C

x

x

x

0   1
miles

Oakland

80   24   680

Lake Shasta

Lake Shasta, a large reservoir, provides a wide variety of angling, including rainbow and brown trout, smallmouth and largemouth bass, panfish and king salmon. The lake, which is basically 4 flooded river canyons, is 35 miles long and has about 365 miles of shoreline. Maximum lake depth is slightly over 500 feet. There are a number of full service marinas(many of which rent houseboats) and campgrounds on the lake. Often, one or more families rent a houseboat, and "bring along" their fishing boat for angling and waterskiing.

Fishing Seasons   (+=good, -=fair)

Species	J	F	M	A	M	J	J	A	S	O	N	D
Trout	+	+	+	+	-	-	-	-	-	-	+	+
Salmon	+	+	+	+	-	-	-	-	-	-	+	+
Bass	-	+	+	+	-	-	-	-		+	+	
Catfish						-	-	-	-	-		
Panfish		-	-	-	-	-	-	-	-	-		

Fishing Tips

Trolling is the most productive trout and salmon approach. Popular offerings include nightcrawlers, Speedy Shiners, Z-Rays and Kastmasters. Trout anglers often use a combination marsh-mallow-nightcrawler-salmon egg on a sliding sinker rig. The marshmallow "floats" the entire combination. Shasta doesn't have a lot of the cover and structures that typifies many largemouth bass lakes. But, smallmouth and some largemouth bass can be found in coves and near rocky points throughout the lake. Live bait, plastic worms, spinnerbaits, crankbaits and jigs all work depending on the time of day, time of year and location. Try a variety of offerings. Shore fishing is good in campgrounds and near marinas throughout the lake.

Information/Bait/Tackle

There are numerous sources of fishing information, and bait and tackle at Lake Shasta. Many of the resorts and marinas, as well as several sporting goods stores, are anxious to provide information and supplies.

Marinas and Launch Ramps

Lake Shasta has a wide variety of full service marinas and public and private launch ramps. The Chamber of Commerce has information at (916)275-1587.

LAKE SHASTA

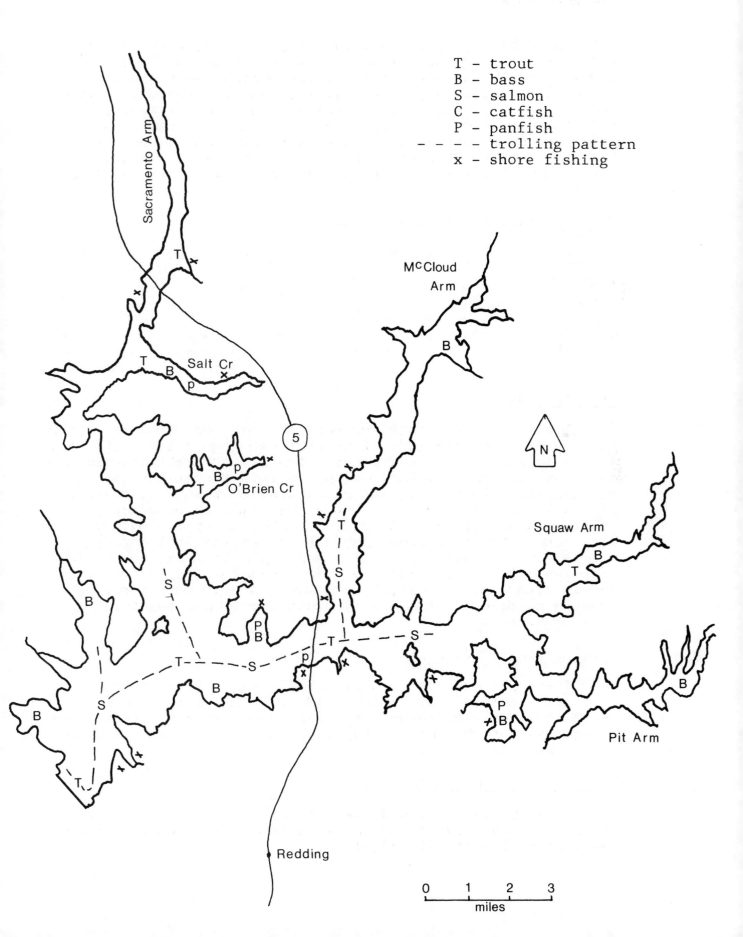

T – trout
B – bass
S – salmon
C – catfish
P – panfish
– – – – trolling pattern
x – shore fishing

Lake Tahoe

Tahoe is a very good, unique Northern California fishery. It is a large(22 miles by 12 miles, 1650 feet deep), high altitude(6230 feet) natural lake. The dominate native trout(a cutthroat) was commercially netted into extinction decades ago. Now Mackinaw Lake trout, rainbow trout and kokanee salmon are the primary fisheries. An occassional brown trout is also caught. Launch ramps, full service marinas and all other types of recreational facilities are widely available in all sections of the lake. A California or Nevada fishing license is required.

Fishing Seasons   (+=good, -=fair)

Species	J	F	M	A	M	J	J	A	S	O	N	D
Mackinaw	+	+	+	+	-	-			-	-	+	+
Browns	-	-	+	+	+	-	-	-	-	+	+	-
Rainbow	+	+	+	+	+	+	+	-	-	+	+	+
Kokanee					-	+	+	+	-			

Fishing Tips

Mackinaw are the prize catch at Tahoe. Rainbow and browns are usually caught by anglers seeking Mackinaw. Mackinaw average 2-6 pounds(about the same as the rainbow) but many are caught in the 6-10 pound range and some fish are caught weighing up to 50 pounds. Trolling with live minnows(from Lake Tahoe), J-Plugs or Flatfish behind flashers is the established technique. Light-colored plugs(silver or bluish) are preferred. Sometimes Mackinaw trolling is done as deep as 200 feet right near the bottom over a structure or a shelf. Kokanee are caught using standard kokanee rigs. Kokanee in the 2-3 pound range are not uncommon. Shore fishing for trout is popular using salmon eggs, nightcrawlers and spinners.

Information/Bait/Tackle

There are numerous sources of fishing information, bait and tackle at Lake Tahoe. Many of the resorts and marinas, as well as several sporting goods stores are anxious to provide information and supplies.

Marinas and Launch Ramps

Lake Tahoe has over 20 marinas and launch ramps, located all around the shoreline.

LAKE TAHOE

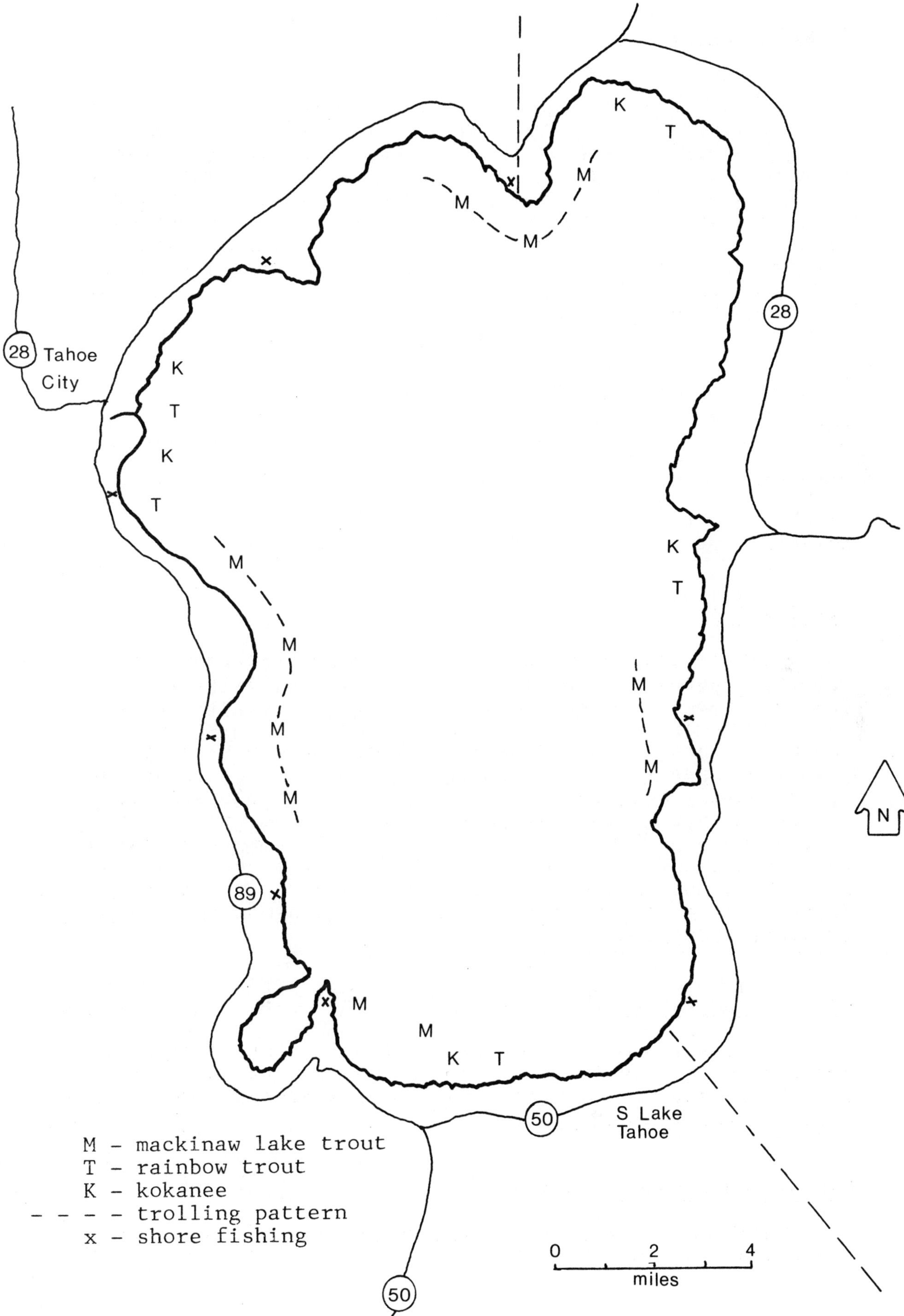

K
T
M
M
M
x

x

28 Tahoe
City

K
T
K
T
M

M

M

28

K
T

M
x
M

x

89 x

x M
M
K T

x

50 S Lake
Tahoe

M – mackinaw lake trout
T – rainbow trout
K – kokanee
– – – – trolling pattern
x – shore fishing

0   2   4
        miles

50

N

Trinity Lake

Trinity Lake is an excellent trout lake. Bass fishing is also very good, particularly for smallmouth bass. But, the amount of cover preferred by largemouth is limited. Trinity is a large lake. It is 22 miles long and has about 145 miles of shoreline. The lake has complete resort, boating and camping facilities.

Fishing Seasons   (+=good, -=fair)

Species	J	F	M	A	M	J	J	A	S	O	N	D
Trout		-	-	+	+	+	+	-	-	-	-	
Kokanee			-	-	-	+	+	+	+	+		
Bass	+	+	+	+	+	+	-	-	-			
Salmon		-	-	-	-	+	+	+	+	+	+	
Panfish		-	-	-	-	-	-	-	-	-	-	

Fishing Tips

Smallmouth bass fishing in Trinity is concentrated at rocky points and outcroppings. Another good bass structure to look for is the underwater, shallow water plateaus or shelfs that are most often found off shore of relatively level campgrounds. An example of an area like this is the gentle slope from Wyntoon Camp North, near Trinity Center. This area which goes on for a mile or more, also has some stumps, so it can be productive for largemouth. In early spring, trout can be found most often near or in the major feeder streams of the lake. In late spring and early summer, trout are often near the drop-off of the shallow shelfs. Late summer-early fall trolling is usually productive at 30-40 feet.

Information/Bait/Tackle

There are numerous sources of fishing information, bait and tackle at Trinity Lake. Many of the resorts and marinas, as well as several sporting goods stores are anxious to provide information and supplies.

Marinas and Launch Ramps

There are eight launch ramps on Trinity Lake. Most are on the east shore. Full service marinas, including boat rental, are available.

TRINITY LAKE

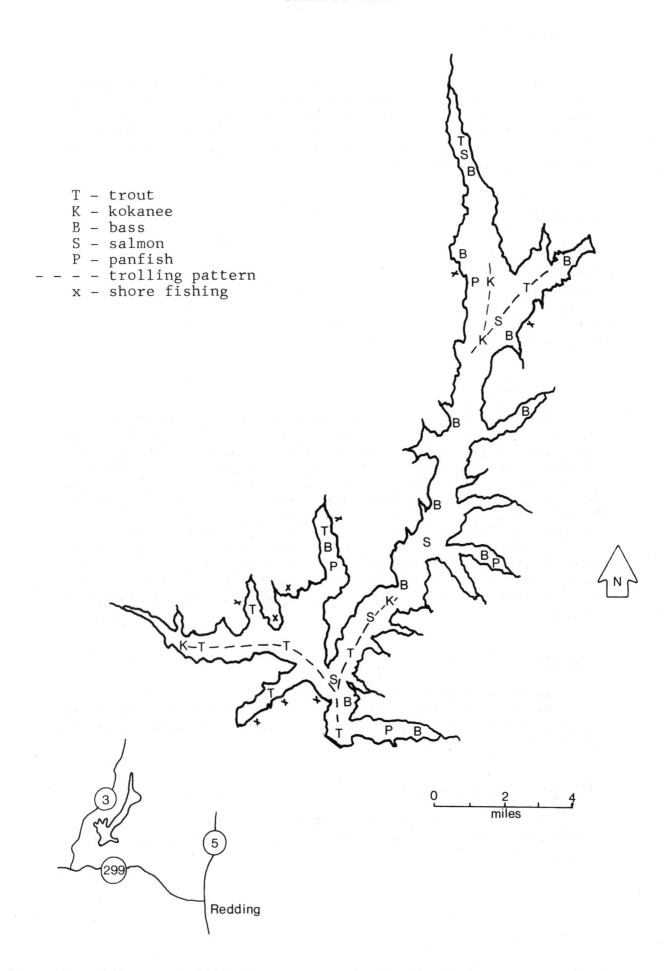

T – trout
K – kokanee
B – bass
S – salmon
P – panfish
– – – – trolling pattern
x – shore fishing

N

0   2   4
miles

3

5

299

Redding

RIVER and STREAM FISHING

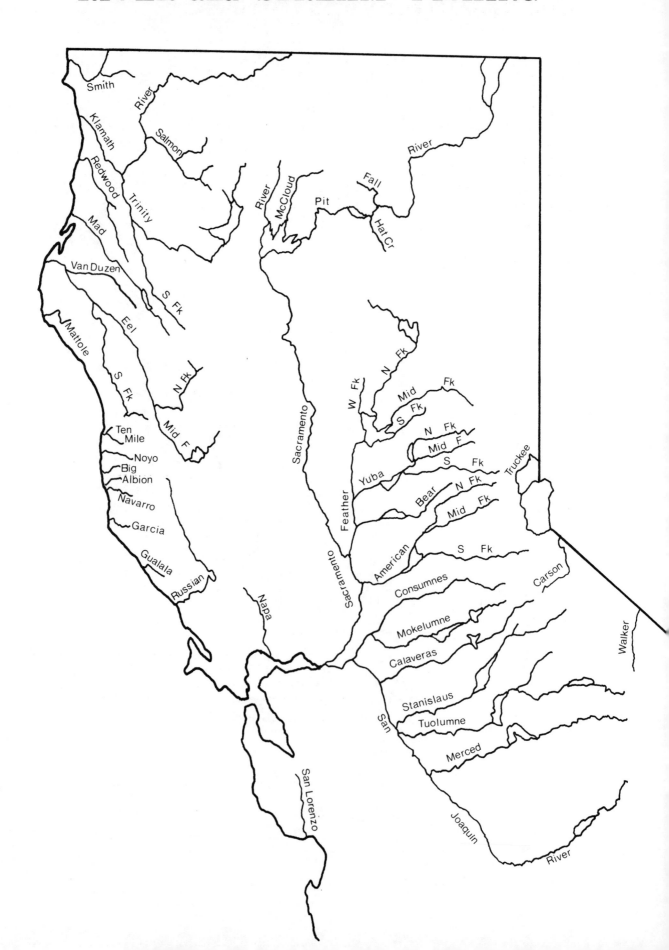

Coastal Rivers and Streams

California anglers are blessed with some of the best coastal fishing streams in the world. Sure fishing in these waters is not what is was 50 years ago, but, it is still good and improving because of the efforts of a number of agencies, groups and individuals. The Klamath, Trinity, Smith and Eel, as well as a number of lesser-known rivers and streams, from the Oregon border south to San Francisco Bay, provide abundant opportunity for steelhead and salmon fishing. In fact, many of these rivers and streams are synonymous with steelhead fishing.

Fishing Seasons (+=good, -=fair)

Species	J	F	M	A	M	J	J	A	S	O	N	D
Steelhead	+	+	+	-				-	-	+	+	+
Salmon							-	+	+	+	+	-

Fishing Tips

Certain streams(Klamath, Eel, Trinity, for example) have some steelhead in them all year, and summer fishing is permitted(see regulations) in some. But, the major run of large fish(steelhead - 8 pounds and up, salmon - average about 20 pounds) takes place in the fall and winter months. This is prime fishing time. Actually migrating fish begin to show in July and August. But good fishing doesn't start in the Trinity and Klamath until September. Fishing in streams with lower summer flow(like the Eel and Russian) doesn't really start until the first heavy rains of the season. Timing is critical to successful steelhead and salmon fishing. The weather, stream flow volume and clarity, and many other factors can effect the bite. Knowledgeable fishermen use the telephone to gauge conditions on various streams and then, once fishing, they're flexible enough to move around if fish aren't being caught. Some experienced fishermen, if need be, call ahead for fishing reports and then drive. Two hours driving might be more productive than two hour fishing.

Eel River

The Eel River is an extremely long coastal stream with several branches. All the opportunities along this river present the same problem; where is the best place to fish at a given time? Steelhead are in the Eel and its branches all fall and winter, but locating them is not always easy in a long river.

One good spot for a visitor to fish is the tidal area. Steelhead are here as early as Labor Day. The key in this section is to keep moving until you find the fish. Access is good, for boat and by foot. Access is also good all along the Eel from the ocean up to the South Fork, in Humboldt Redwoods State Park, and there are many fishing opportunities. But, from this point up-river, the accessibility of the main body of the Eel River is poor. This continues all the way to near its headwaters. But near the headwaters, particularly in the stretch between Thomas Creek and the Van Arsdale Dam, late season steelhead fishing is accessible and productive. The area is about 5 miles out of Potter Valley.

Access is excellent all along the South Fork of the Eel as it passes through Humboldt State Park and farther south, since it continues to parallel Hwy. 101. Finally, the North Fork of the Eel presents serious access problems. The main stream of the Eel has peek steelhead fishing from December through February. Eel River steelhead are large, averaging 8-14 pounds.

Klamath River

The mighty Klamath River, more than 200 miles long, from the ocean to the Oregon border, provides a wide variety of steelhead and salmon fishing experiences. The lower Klamath, which runs from Weitchpec at the mouth of the Trinity(a tributary of the Klamath) to the ocean is the largest and probably the most heavily fished. The waters here average about 100-200 feet wide. To adequately cover this high, deep stream most anglers use 9 foot rods. Longer surf casting rods are used at the mouth of the river during the salmon run. The bulk of the salmon taken from the Klamath come from the lower Klamath during the fall. Activity begins in July, and is at its peak during August, September and October. Trolling near the deep channels at the mouth of the river is often congested. Farther upstream, salmon are most often taken at tributary inflows. Some of the best are Blue Creek, Trinity River, Bluff Creek, Salmon River, Scott River and Shasta River.

Steelhead anglers crowd the accessible portion of the 40 mile stretch of the Lower Klamath through the fall and winter. Boats are used by many to either backtroll or move to a section of run not accessible by foot, for a less hectic shore fishing experience.

The Middle Klamath, between Weitchpec and the mouth of Scott River at Hamburg, provides many foot-accessible areas for shore fishing(from state 96). The water is narrower here and many anglers use light to medium spinner tackle (e.g. a 7 foot rod) normally associated with trout fishing.

From Scott River up to Shasta River(near I-5) the Klamath also provides good foot access. From I-5 up to the Oregon border, boat fishing predominates. The river here runs primarily through private property and much of this is posted. Salmon usually reach this stretch of the Klamath in early October, with the steelhead arriving a week or so later.

Russian River

The Russian River is a good steelhead stream. Good runs of steelhead enter the river from November through February. It flows through more gentle terrain than the streams farther north, and is fished both from shore and by boat. Access is good along most of the river, but private property prevents direct access to some good pools. Early season anglers find good access at the tidal section of the Russian, through Goat Rock State Beach. A good, late season spot is between Cloverdale and Hopland. Here Hwy. 101 crosses the river twice and provides many good pull-off spots. The Squaw Rock stretch is particularly productive. Fish the deep holes.

The Russian also has striped bass and shad runs. May is usually prime time for shad. One of the best spots for shad is the pool below the Summer Dam at Healdsburg, especially in the latter weeks of May.

Smith River

The Smith is the northernmost of California's major steelhead streams. One desirable feature of the Smith, besides the number and large size of its steelhead, is the quickness with which if clears after a winter storm. Often it is clear and fishable within a few days following most significant storms. Some other streams take up to two weeks to clear. The Smith clears so quickly because most of its streambed is solid rock.

From September on, large salmon run in the Smith. Steelhead usually begin in force in November and run through April. The most productive and legendary portion of the Smith is between the 101 bridge and the 199 bridge. Many large steelhead are taken in this 7-8 mile long stretch. Many holes provide excellent holding waters for salmon and steelhead. The Smith is a short river and its access points on the Middle Fork, along Hwy. 199, can be reached quickly. Small boats are launched just below the 101 bridge.

Trinity River

The Trinity River is an excellent steelhead and salmon stream. And the main river, between Weitchpec and Junction City is noteworthy because of its excellent access since Hwy. 299 parallels the Trinity along much of its course. And not only is it possible to get to and park near a good location, but the climb down to the river often is comfortable. Anglers use 199 to move along the river to find the area where steelhead are being taken. It's possible to cover many promising spots along the river in as little as 2 days.

The South Fork of the Trinity offers excellent fishing but access is extremely limited, although there is a road to Hyampon and vicinity. Above the North Fork of the Trinity the main branch changes. It is very brushy, and even the streambed has reeds, willows, etc. This makes fly fishing very difficult. This condition is a result of the dams upstream(at Trinity Lake and Lewiston Lake) which prevent flood level flows from flushing the streambed.

Other Steelhead Streams

Besides the major steelhead and salmon rivers detailed in this section, there are streams that provide good steelhead fishing in the fall-winter months. These include;

- . Redwood Creek - A short stream in Humboldt County.

- . Mad River - Another short but productive stream in Humboldt County.

- . Salmon River - Tributary of the Klamath runs in Siskiyou County.

- . Scott River - Another tributary of the Klamath which runs in Siskiyou County.

- . Van Duzen River - A tributary of the main Eel River in Humboldt County.

- . Mattole River - A fine coastal stream in Humboldt County.

- . Tenmile River - A short coastal stream in Northern Mendocino County.

- . Noyo River - A coastal stream just south of Tenmile River.

- . Big River - Coastal stream in central Mendocino County.

- . Albion River - Coastal stream in central Mendocino County

- . Navarro River - Coastal stream in central Mendocino County.

- . Garcia River - Coastal stream in central Mendocino County.

- . Gualala River - Coastal stream in central Mendocino County.

• San Lorenzo River – Coastal stream in Santa Cruz County.

A summary of salmon and steelhead streams is provided below;

SALMON AND STEELHEAD PORTS AND STREAMS

Coastal Streams and Their Tributaries; Main Streams Listed From North to South, Tributaries Listed From Upstream Down

Stream	Steel-head	Silver Salmon	King Salmon	Time of Salmon and Steelhead Runs and Other Comments
SMITH RIVER	Yes	Yes	Yes	At the mouth and in the lagoon there is a large skiff fishery. King salmon are the biggest attraction. Best fishing for kings is late Sept. through Oct.; silvers run about a month later. Some steelhead are taken in the lagoon. Sea-run cutthroat fishing fall, winter, and spring; best March through May. Above the lagoon fishing for salmon, steelhead, and cutthroat fall and winter. Most of the Smith system is in canyons.
KLAMATH RIVER	Yes	Yes	Yes	At the mouth and in the lagoon there is a large skiff fishery for king salmon, best in Aug. and Sept.; silvers late Sept. through Oct.; sea-run cutthroat fishing Sept. through April; best in March and April. Fall steelhead run is best in the lower river in Aug. and Sept.; about a month later near Copco Dam. Some summer steelhead available. Winter steelhead best in Jan. and Feb.; but high water usually bothers fishermen. Upriver salmon fishing fair in fall.
SCOTT RIVER	Yes	Yes	Yes	Runs through farming country. Much of the bottom has been gold dredged. Salmon and steelhead in fall. Some winter steelhead. Canyon below farming area is best.
SALMON RIVER	Yes	Yes	Yes	Some summer steelhead. Good steelhead and salmon stream in the fall. The mouth of the Salmon River is an especially good spot.
Wooley Creek	Yes		Yes	Spring-run salmon, summer steelhead, no winter fishing, no roads.
TRINITY RIVER	Yes	Yes	Yes	Spring-run king salmon available near Lewiston May through summer. Kings also available through most of the river in the fall. Some silver salmon in the lower parts of the Trinity. Some summer steelhead. Best steelhead fishing from the first fall rains through the winter.
SOUTH FORK TRINITY RIVER	Yes	Yes	Yes	Some spring-run king salmon, good fall run of kings. Some silvers in lower part of South Fork. Steelhead in fall and winter.
REDWOOD CREEK	Yes	Yes	Yes	Best in fall and winter. A dry fall may delay the runs. Good sea-run cutthroat fishing in tidewater fall, winter, and early spring.
Little River	Yes	Yes		Fall and winter—runs start after first heavy rains.
MAD RIVER	Yes	Yes	Yes	Fall and winter. A dry fall may delay the runs.
Elk River	Yes	Yes	Few	Fall and winter—runs start after first heavy rains.
EEL RIVER	Yes	Yes	Yes	Trolling for king salmon in tidewater late Aug. through Oct. Kings are caught further upstream fall and winter. Half-pounder fishing below the Van Duzen late summer and early fall. Larger steelhead below the Van Duzen in the fall. Winter fishing for steelhead throughout the river system.
MIDDLE FORK EEL RIVER	Yes		Yes	Salmon and steelhead fishing fall and winter. Some summer steelhead near Covelo and above.
SOUTH FORK EEL RIVER	Yes	Yes	Yes	Fall and winter fishing for steelhead and salmon.
VAN DUZEN RIVER	Yes	Yes	Yes	Fall and winter fishing for steelhead and salmon. Some summer steelhead above Bridgeville.
Bear River	Yes	Yes	Yes	November or later, depending on rains.
MATTOLE RIVER	Yes	Yes	Yes	November or later, depending on rains.
TEN MILE RIVER	Yes	Yes		November or later, depending on rains.
NOYO RIVER	Yes	Yes		November or later, depending on rains.
BIG RIVER	Yes	Yes		November or later, depending on rains.
ALBION RIVER	Yes	Yes		November or later, depending on rains.
NAVARRO RIVER	Yes	Yes		November or later, depending on rains.
Greenwood Creek	Yes			November or later, depending on rains.
Alder Creek	Yes			November or later, depending on rains.
Brush Creek	Yes			November or later, depending on rains.
GARCIA RIVER	Yes	Yes	Few	November or later, depending on rains.
GUALALA RIVER	Yes	Yes		November or later, depending on rains.
RUSSIAN RIVER	Yes	Yes		Fall and winter—runs apt to be delayed by late rains. Silver salmon confined roughly to lower 40 miles of river.
Salmon Creek	Yes	Yes		Fall and winter—depending on rains and water flow.
Walker Creek	Yes	Yes		Fall and winter—depending on rains and water flow.
PAPERMILL CREEK	Yes	Yes		Fall and winter—depending on rains and water flow.
NAPA RIVER	Yes			Fall and winter—runs start after first heavy rains.
Alameda Creek	Yes			Late fall and winter—Recommended only for local people.
San Gregorio Creek	Yes			Late fall and winter—Recommended only for local people.
Pescadero Creek	Yes	Few		Late fall and winter—Recommended only for local people.
Scott Creek	Yes	Few		Late fall and winter—Recommended only for local people.
SAN LORENZO RIVER	Yes	Few		Fall and winter—depending on rains and water flow.
Soquel Creek	Yes	Few		Late fall and winter—Recommended only for local people.
Pajaro River	Yes			Late fall and winter—Recommended only for local people.
CARMEL RIVER	Yes			Fall and winter—depending on rains and water flow.
BIG SUR RIVER	Yes			Fall and winter—depending on rains and water flow.

Central Valley Rivers

The central Valley rivers of Northern California offer some of the finest fishing in the entire state. The most productive waters are the Sacramento River and its tributaries(American, Feather and Yuba Rivers). In these waters fishing is almost a year-round activity. There's steelhead and salmon beginning in late summer and running through winter. Striped bass, sturgeon and shad make spawning runs into the Sacramento system in the spring. And if the migratory fish aren't enough, there's still catfishing, smallmouth bass, rainbow and brown trout fishing in these rivers.

Fishing Seasons   (+=good, -=fair)

Species	J	F	M	A	M	J	J	A	S	O	N	D
Salmon	+	+	+	-	-	-		-	+	+	+	+
Steelhead	+	+	-					-	-	+	+	+
Striper	+	+	+	-	-	-		-	-	+	+	
Sturgeon	+	+	-	-	-	-	-	-	-	-	−	+
Shad			-	+	+	-						

Fishing Tips

The key to successful fishing in these rivers is to be there when the action is hot. Salmon, steelhead, striper, sturgeon and shad are migrating through the Central Valley Rivers to get to their spawning grounds. So they're on the move. In addition, most of the best fishing takes place during the rainy season, so stream conditions can change rapidly. Keep in touch with fishing tackle stores, fishing guide services and bait shops, in the stretches of river you want to fish, for up-to-date information. Shore fishing is possible in selected areas, but boats are used by many to increase coverage and to reach spots that flow through the many farms and ranches. But boating these rivers during high water flow months requires experience and skill.

American River

The American offers one of the best metropolitan angling experiences in the entire United States. It flows
about 22 miles from the Nimbus Dam in Fair Oaks to its confluence with the Sacramento River, just north of downtown
Sacramento. Salmon, steelhead, striper and shad visit the
river, and trout, smallmouth bass and catfish make it their
permanent home.

Many anglers use drift boats, putting in near the Nimbus Basin. These boaters fish holes such as Upper Sunrise,
Bridge Street, Lower Sunrise, Sacramento Bar, Rossmoor Bar
and the mouth at Sacramento. But the American also offers
great shore fishing possibilities. Some of the best spots
are the Nimbus Basin, Sailor Bar Park, Upper and Lower Sunrise, Rossmoor Bar, Goethe Park, the end of Arden Way, Watt
Avenue bridge , Howe Avenue bridge, Paradise Beach, the area
behind Cal Expo and the Discovery Park area.

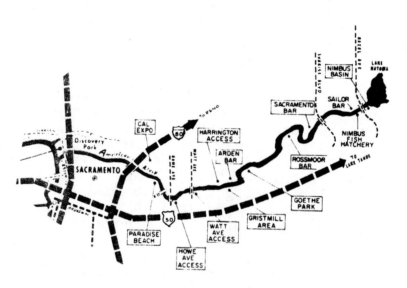

There is a closure on the American River from Nimbus
Basin downstream about 8 miles to just below Hoffman Park
from November 1st to January 1st. This closure allows

salmon and steelhead to spawn in the upper river during these months. Salmon fishing is usually best before the closure and the larger steelhead are usually taken after the closure. A shad and striper hot spot is the Discovery Park Area. Two strains of steelhead use the American. The Coleman strain usually makes its way up the American from September and November. The large Eel River strain is found in the river from December and March.

Feather and Yuba River

The lower Feather River flows from the Lake Oroville reservoir dam in Oroville down to its confluence with the Sacramento River at Verona. It offers good salmon, steelhead, striper and shad fishing. The fall salmon run usually begins in early September and lasts for 2-3 months. Due to private property restrictions, most anglers fish with boats from Verona up to Shanghai Bend rapids, south of the Yuba River confluence. Good boat fishing spots south of Yuba City include deep holes below the rapids of Boyd's Pump, above the rapids, above the mouth of the Yuba River, above and below Star Bend. Above Yube City two good areas are the Car Body Hole and the Long Hole.

Bank anglers do well just below and above Shanghai Bend. Another good shore fishing area is in the riffles from the Gridley Bridge up to Thermolito Afterbay. Just downstream of the Thermolito outlet is a good spot to cast large, weighted spinners. The Feather is closed to salmon angling from Honicut Creek upstream to the Highway 70 bridge in Oroville from mid-October to years end. And the Feather is closed to all fishing from the Highway 70 bridge to Table Mountain Blvd. from September to December.

Striper and shad are at their peak in the Feather in May. Shad and steelhead are good in the Yuba River. Good shore access is available from its mouth up to the Highway 20 bridge.

Sacramento River

About 60% of all the salmon caught off the coast of Northern California were spawned in the Lower Sacramento River. It runs from Redding to Sacramento. The Sacramento hosts 4 salmon runs each year, and with the right conditions, salmon can be caught here during any season. But the fall-winter run is the biggest. Good fishing can begin in August, with catches of 10-20 pounders. Larger salmon(40 pounders aren't uncommon) are more frequent in the winter months.

The prime salmon fishing in the Sacramento is from Los Molinos north to the cut-off line at the Deschutes Road bridge, near Anderson(just south of Redding). In this section of river, bank access is limited by private property, so most anglers use boats. Public launch ramps are available. Guide services are very active here. A list is available from the Shasta-Cascade Wonderland Association in Redding(916-243-2643). Backtrolling is the most common technique. Salmon and steelhead fishing is also good all the way down the river to the city of Sacramento. Colusa, Meridian, Knight's Landing, Verona are all fishing centers. In the city of Sacramento, two good fishing spots are Miller Park and the Government Docks.

Striper action on the Sacramento extends from Rio Vista all the way up to Colusa-Princeton. Shad fishing on the Sacramento extends from above Freeport to the mouth of the American in Sacramento, to the mouth of the Feather at Verona and all the way up to Los Molinos. Most fishing takes place from bars using waders, or from boats. A winter spawning hot spot for sturgeon is the Princeton-Colusa-Meridian section of the Sacramento. The best shore fishing access points on the Sacramento are at and north of Woodson Bridge State Recreation area near Corning.

Mountain Rivers and Streams

Mountain river and stream fishing in Northern California means trout fishing. Trout fishing takes the angler to some of the most beautiful spots in this most beautiful state. This point was eloquently made back in 1894 when David Starr Jordan, writing at the conclusion of a State Fish Commission report, said, "In writing on the trout of California, one does not willingly lay down the pen at the end. The most beautiful of fishes, the most charming of lands, where the two are connected, one wishes to say something better of them than has been said. It is with regret that he lets fall the pen in confession of inability to say it."

Much has changed in California in the last 90 or so years. But the beauty of many of our mountain streams and of our trout has not. In this section a wide variety of enriching and productive trout fishing locations are profiled.

Fishing Tips

With some variation, the stream trout season in Northern California runs from the last Saturday in April through November 15(check regulations). The success of a stream fishing experience during this open season depends on many factors including, the amount of snowfall, the runoff, timing of insect hatches, weather patterns, etc.

Generally, stream trout fishing is better in the spring and fall, than it is in the summer. But summer fishing is often productive. When summer comes on, veteran anglers follow 60-65° water temperature up to higher elevations as backroads become passable. In July and August, a good spot is the cool tailwaters below dams.

One approach that always seems to produce more and larger trout is to contradict human nature. Most anglers park at a stream access point, walk to the water and begin to fish. So the pros have found that it's always better to hike for say 15 minutes along a stream before fishing. This will get you beyond the overworked and underpopulated spots into some really good fishing action.

Once fishing in a stream, the most productive anglers aren't afraid to get into the water. Don't just wade around the edges and fish from convenient spots. Get in the water with chest waders, if necessary, and move to the spots that provide access to the most likely holes.

Burney Basin Trout

Burney Basin is located in Shasta County, surrounding the town of Burney, about 50 miles east of Redding on Highway 299. Hat Creek and Fall River, in this basin, are considered among the best trout streams in the west.

Hat Creek is divided into two portions. The 3.5 miles of Lower Hat Creek(from Power House No. 2 to Lake Britton) is a designated wild trout stream. Here, only flies and lures with a single barbless hook are allowed, and a two-fish 18" minimum size limit is in effect. Trout hooked here average between 10-16" with an occassional one in the 20-24" range. There are some lunker browns over 10 pounds! Access is very good. Park where 299 crosses the creek and walk upstream or downstream. Fly fishing is very popular here. This is a broad, meadow stream. Wading is popular.

Upper Hat Creek is well stocked with hatchery fish. Most trout caught are in the 8-11" range. This stream from above Baum Lake runs along Highway 89 and access is good. A popular access is Big Pine Campground. Bait fishing(worms, salmon eggs, and crickets) is most productive.

Another well stocked and productive stream in the area is Burney Creek. A PG&E campground is available at Cassel Park. Camping is also available in McArthur-Burney Falls State Park at Lake Britton.

Fall River is a wild trout stream, like Lower Hat Creek. But, since it runs mostly through private property, it is fished using float tubes or electric powered small boats. The fish are big here, many weighing from 5-8 pounds. Fly fishing is most popular. There are two lodges that provide access if you stay with them, and there is public access at the Cal Trout Boat Launch at Island Bridge.

Below, where Tule River meets Fall River, there are no tackle restrictions. Boats can be launched at the PG&E dredge access at the intersection of Glenburn and McArthur roads. Good fishing for rainbow, up to 7 pounds can be had on nightcrawlers, Rebels, Kastmasters and Panther Martins, as well as flys.

More information on this excellent trout fishing is available from the Burney Basin Chamber of Commerce, Box 36, Burney, CA 96013 (1-800-831-6259).

Emigrant Wilderness Trout

Emigrant Wilderness, located south of Highway 108, the Sonora Pass, in Tuolumne County, is a beautiful and unique area, with breathtaking scenery. There is excellent trout fishing in its many streams and lakes.

If you and your family or friends like to combine a backpacking trip with trout fishing, this may be the place for you. But don't plan on a late spring trip. Mother nature usually doesn't open these waters until June, and it may be July before some trails are clear of snow. Most lakes are ice-free by mid-June.

Access to Emigrant is through the Pinecrest Lake-Dodge Ridge area at Strawberry. There are about 5 different trailheads in this area plus a pack station. Top streams include Summit Creek above Relief Reservoir, Lily Creek, and Horsemeadow Creek. A good pristine lake zone is in the southwestern portion of the wilderness. Rosasco, Hyatt, Pingree, Big, Yellowhammer, and Lord Meadow lakes. Also the stream between Layton and Yellowhammer lakes is a good producer.

Emigrant Wilderness is a rugged area. Only experienced backpackers should explore this area. Information is available from Summit Ranger Station, USFS Star Route, Box 1295, Sonora, CA 95370 (209-965-3434).

Sacramento and McCloud River Trout

These are two great trout streams. Both are located just north of Lake Shasta, and, in fact, flow into this major reservoir.

The Upper Sacramento just about parallels I-5 from Lake Siskiyou to Lake Shasta. This major highway, along with accompanying railroad tracks, provides very good access to the Upper Sacramento. This is a good-sized river with enticing riffles, deep pools, and many trophy-sized rainbow and brown trout. Trout catches up to 18" are not all that unusual here.

Both bait(especially nightcrawlers), spinner and fly fishing are great on the Upper Sacramento. Some fly fishing devotees compare the Upper Sacramento with the prime fly streams of Montana and Wyoming. It has a very diverse hatch of aquatic insects from July to mid-October. Camping and day-use facilities are available right along the river.

The McCloud runs parallel to Highway 89 east of McCloud and then south to Lake McCloud and finally into Lake Shasta. It offers a variety of trout fishing alternatives. First, there is the portion that runs about a mile south of Highway 89. There is good access near Fowler Camp about 5 miles east of the town of McCloud. Other secondary roads off of 89 can also be used. This is a meadow stream that runs for miles. Flow is gentle and fishermen wade here in summer without waders. Trout are planted and the limit is 10 fish. Both spinning and fly fishing are good.

A second alternative is to fish the stretch just south of the McCloud Dam. It can be reached by taking Squaw Valley Road about 12 miles out of the town of McCloud. In this 6.5 mile stretch only artifical lures and flys may be used and the limit is two fish per day. Access is via Ash Camp, about a mile downstream from the dam, on a road on the east side of the river. This is canyon stream with more flow than in the Upper McCloud.

Finally, there is a catch-and -release stretch of the McCloud that begins at the mouth of Ladybug Creek and extends for about 2 miles. Take the road on the west side of the McCloud Lake dam that leads to the Ah-Di-Na Campground. Only artificial lures and flys with barbless, single hooks can be used.

Eastern Sierra Trout

Eastern Sierra streams offer some excellent trout fishing. Good streams include the East Walker, the West Walker, Carson River, Truckee River and the Little Truckee River.

The East Walker, below Bridgeport Lake, near Bridgeport is an excellent stream for large brown trout. Highway

182 parallels this river and provides good access. Other good trout streams in the Bridgeport area include Robinson, Buckeye, and Swauger Creeks. The West Walker which runs along Highway 395 and Highway 180 is also a good stream, but trout are small here compared to the East Walker. However, there is one bonus. The West Walker is easier to wade. The Walkers are usually fishable all summer.

The Truckee River flows from Lake Tahoe, at Tahoe City, along Highway 89 to the town of Truckee and from there along Highway 80 into Nevada. Good spots are at Alpine and Squaw Creek and from Boca exit to Nevada. A popular trout bait on the Truckee is crayfish tails, especially before crayfish come out. Spinners are also productive.

The Little Truckee, one of the better east slope streams, runs above and below Stampede Reservoir, north of the town of Truckee. Upstream of Stampede, along Highway 89 is a good stretch for small spinners.

Trinity Alps Trout

Trout fishing is very good in the Trinity Mountains that are north and west of Trinity Lake. Several types of outings are possible here. If you're fishing and camping on Trinity Lake and have a desire to do some stream fishing for trout, then you're in the right place. Here are some choices;

- Upper Trinity River - This river runs along Highway 3, north of the lake. It and the Little Trinity River, farther upstream, provide good fishing, especially in late spring and fall.

- Coffee Creek - This creek is a tributary of the Upper Trinity River. Access is good via Coffee Creek Road which parallels it. Coffee Creek provides some of the best all-season trout fishing in the area.

- East Fork of Upper Tinity - This stream runs north out of the northwest section of Tinity Lake. It has a generous caddis fly hatch. Some of the best fishing is in the riffles and pools downstream of the access where East Side Road crosses the river.

If you'd rather walk than drive to your trout fishing stream, the Salmon-Trinity Alps Wilderness Area is close by. There is some wonderful stream and lake fishing in this area. Two convenient access points are Stuart Fork near Trinity Alp Resort(Hwy 3) and Big Flat(end of Coffee Creek Road).

Yosemite Trout

Some fine, wild trout fishing can be found thousands of feet above Yosemite Valley floor, in Tuolumne Meadows along Highway 120. Here above Hetch Hetchy Reservoir, the Tuolumne and its branches, the Dana Fork and the Lyell Fork provide abundant brook, brown and rainbow trout in the 6-18" range.

The fishing season is short at this 8600 foot elevation. The waters are still high in June. July is usually good fishing and it peaks in August.

The Tuolumne is easily fished in the Meadows itself as it runs along Highway 120. A mile or so downstream of the meadow the Tuolumne quickens its pace as it falls over granite structure. Fish here and about a miles walk up from the Meadows, in Dana Fork are larger than those caught right in the Meadows. A short drive east on Highway 120 from the Meadows provides access at several points to more of the Dana Fork. Follow the John Muir Trail south from the Meadows to fish the Lyell Fork.

Tuolumne Meadows is a popular tourist and camping area. August is the busiest month. Here is a good place to combine family sightseeing, hiking, campling and trout fishing.

PACIFIC, BAY and DELTA FISHING

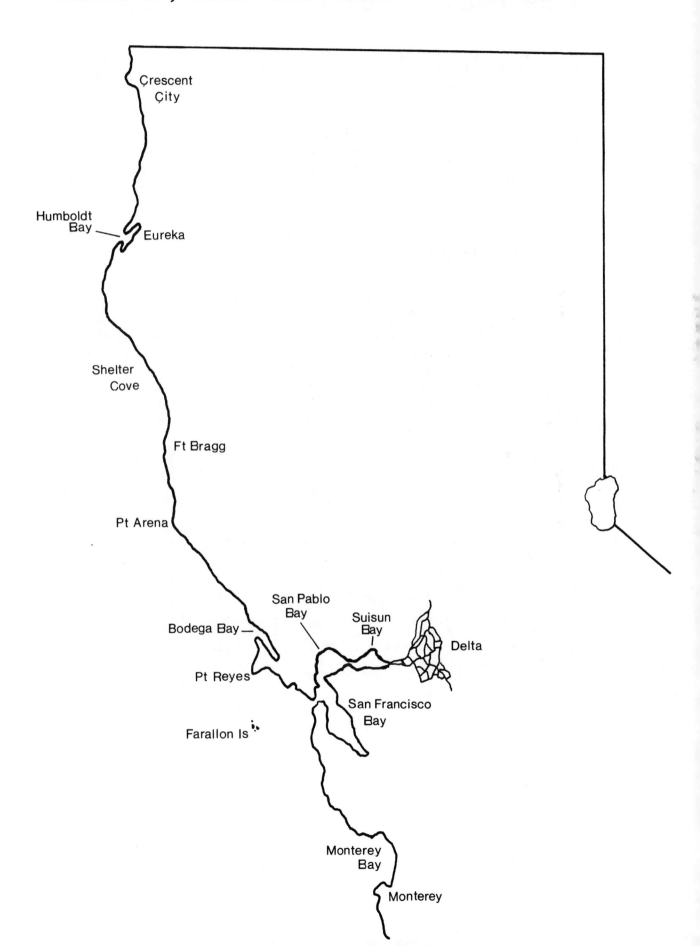

The Pacific Ocean

The coastal waters of the Pacific Ocean offer an immense variety of fishing opportunities. There is salmon trolling, bottom fishing for rock cod and lingcod, albacore fishing 20-30 miles offshore, pier fishing for all kinds of fish depending on location and season and finally, surf fishing for striped bass and perch.

But, ocean fishing can be dangerous. Fishermen are lost every year. Breakers wash anglers off rocks. People fall overboard. Increased winds are foolishly ignored. Equipment fails. But don't let this scare you away from fishing. Do enjoy the marvelous experience of ocean fishing, but be prepared, be careful and error on the side of caution.

Fishing Seasons   (+=good, -=fair)

Species	J	F	M	A	M	J	J	A	S	O	N	D
Salmon		-	-	-	+	+	-	-	-	-		
Rock Cod	-	-	-	-	-	-	-	-	-	-	-	-
Lingcod	+	+	-	-	-	-	-	-	-	+	+	+
Striper						-	+	+	-	-		
Halibut						-	+	+	-			
Albacore							-	+	-			
Abalone				-	-	-		+	+	-	-	
Rock Crab	-	-	-	-	-	-	-	-	-	-	-	-

Fishing Tips

Salmon fishing can get hot anytime during the season, but more predictable is the size of the catch. Bigger salmon move closer to shore starting in July. August and September are the months when most of the twenty pound plus king salmon are taken. Ocean fishing for striper is probably best near shore and in the surf in the Pacifica area, when the anchovies move into shallow water. Halibut can be caught in the shallow waters(as shallow as 10 feet) of ocean bays like Monterey and Tomales. The albacore season is short and unpredictable, so stay alert or you'll miss the season. Rock cod and lingcod can be caught all year. But the best lingcod season is mid-winter when these fish move into shallow water(50-150 feet) to spawn.

Monterey Bay Area Coast

Monterey Bay is an important recreational fishing area, and an impressive number and variety of marine game fish are taken here. Most sport fishing from boats is for bottomfish (particularly rockfishes) although albacore, bonito, and chinook salmon also are landed in season. In some years salmon are abundant in the bay in spring and good fishing may last till late summer. In general, the major marine sport fishes caught from boats and from shore are rockfishes, chinook salmon, California halibut, Pacific sanddab, surfperches, lingcod, kelp greenling, white coraker, and albacore.

The town of Monterey has two public piers, but most fishing takes place from Municipal Pier #2 at the eastern end of the harbor. Here the catch is young bocaccio, blue rockfish, surfperches, jacksmelt, white croaker, and some years, jack mackerel in summer.

Broad sandy beaches rim the coast from the Monterey Peninsula north along the inner curve of the bay all the way to Seacliff State Beach. Most beaches offer excellent fishing for a variety of sandy-shore fishes. Striped bass sometimes are taken by surf casters during the summer along beaches from Monterey north to the Salinas River. All beaches north of the Salinas River offer excellent surf fishing for sand sole, jacksmelt, and surfperches.

At the entrance to Moss Landing harbor, anglers fish from the jetty for surfperches, starry flounder, and occasionally California halibut and striped bass. There is also fishing from shore inside Elkhorn Slough for surfperches plus sharks, rays, sand sole and starry flounder.

The northern end of Seacliff State Beach, near Aptos, has a fishing pier(actually a cement ship) from which anglers catch Pacific sanddab, surfperches, white croaker, jacksmelt, small bocaccio, jack mackerel(during some summers) and an occassional California halibut, starry flounder, lingcod, salmon and steelhead.

Rocky outcroppings and low bluffs begin to interrupt sandy beaches north of Aptos, and rocky-shore fishes start to appear in the angler's catch, replacing sandy-shore

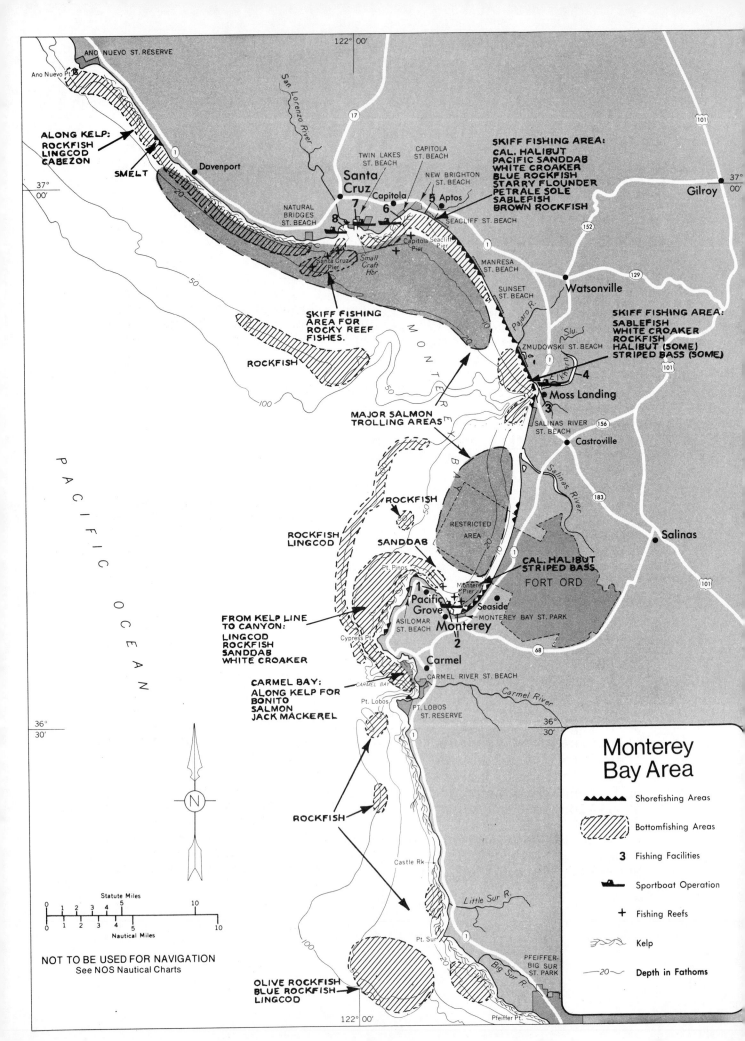

ANO NUEVO ST. RESERVE

Ano Nuevo Pt.

ALONG KELP:
ROCKFISH
LINGCOD
CABEZON

SMELT

Davenport

37° 00'

TWIN LAKES
ST. BEACH

NEW BRIGHTON
ST. BEACH

CAPITOLA
ST. BEACH

Santa Cruz

Capitola

Aptos

NATURAL
BRIDGES
ST. BEACH

7

6

5

8

SEACLIFF ST. BEACH

Capitola
Pier

Seacliff
Pier

Santa Cruz Pier

Small
Craft
Hbr.

SKIFF FISHING AREA:
CAL. HALIBUT
PACIFIC SANDDAB
WHITE CROAKER
BLUE ROCKFISH
STARRY FLOUNDER
PETRALE SOLE
SABLEFISH
BROWN ROCKFISH

Gilroy

37°
00'

MANRESA
ST. BEACH

SKIFF FISHING
AREA FOR
ROCKY REEF
FISHES.

SUNSET
ST. BEACH

Watsonville

ROCKFISH

Pajaro R.

M O N T E R E Y

Slu.

ZMUDOWSKI ST. BEACH

SKIFF FISHING AREA:
SABLEFISH
WHITE CROAKER
ROCKFISH
HALIBUT (SOME)
STRIPED BASS (SOME)

4

Moss Landing

3

MAJOR SALMON
TROLLING AREAS

SALINAS RIVER
ST. BEACH

Castroville

Salinas River

P A C I F I C

ROCKFISH

ROCKFISH
LINGCOD

ROCKFISH

SANDDAB

RESTRICTED
AREA

Salinas

CAL. HALIBUT
STRIPED BASS

FORT ORD

Pt. Pinos

1

Monterey
Pier

O C E A N

FROM KELP LINE
TO CANYON:
LINGCOD
ROCKFISH
SANDDAB
WHITE CROAKER

Pacific
Grove

ASILOMAR
ST. BEACH

Monterey

Seaside

MONTEREY BAY ST. PARK

2

Cypress Pt.

CARMEL BAY:
ALONG KELP FOR
BONITO
SALMON
JACK MACKEREL

CARMEL BAY

Carmel

CARMEL RIVER ST. BEACH

36°
30'

36°
30'

Pt. Lobos

PT. LOBOS
ST. RESERVE

Carmel River

ROCKFISH

Castle Rk.

Little Sur R.

Statute Miles
0 1 2 3 4 5   10

0 1 2 3 4 5   10
Nautical Miles

N

Pt. Sur

PFEIFFER-
BIG SUR
ST. PARK

NOT TO BE USED FOR NAVIGATION
See NOS Nautical Charts

OLIVE ROCKFISH
BLUE ROCKFISH
LINGCOD

Pfeiffer Pt.

122° 00'

Monterey
Bay Area

▲▲▲▲ Shorefishing Areas

▨▨ Bottomfishing Areas

3 Fishing Facilities

🚤 Sportboat Operation

+ Fishing Reefs

〰〰 Kelp

—20— Depth in Fathoms

fishes in importance as one proceeds westward. At the Capitola pier, which is mostly over sandy bottom, the usual fare
is white croaker, jacksmelt, small bocaccio, surfperches and
cabezon.

To the west at the Santa Cruz pier, anglers catch both
rocky and sandy shore fishes such as surfperches, lingcod,
cabezon, young bocaccio, kelp rockfish, topsmelt, jacksmelt,
staghorn sculpin, skates, Pacific sanddab, sand sole, starry
flounder, and white croaker. There is an artificial tire
reef under this pier. Rockfishes are taken from Santa Cruz
Small-Craft Harbor jetties, and in some years coho salmon
and steelhead are taken around the mouth of the San Lorenzo
River.

From Natural Bridges State Beach north to Ano Nuevo Pt.
the shoreline changes rather abruptly to a predominantly
rocky coastline, and fog and blustery northwest winds once
again sweep the coast. This rocky shoreline offers excellent
shore fishing for kelp greenling, cabezon, grass rockfish,
and surfperches.

Most of the Monterey Bay area boat catch is made up of
several species of rockfishes, Pacific sanddab, chinook salmon, and lingcod. Most small-boat fishing takes place inside Monterey Bay, although on calm days Monterey anglers
occasionally venture out around the peninsula between Point
Pinos and Cypress Point to fish for lingcod and some of the
nearshore rockfishes, or try their luck in Carmel Bay.

Inside Carmel Bay boats work along the edge of the kelp
for lingcod and rockfishes; sometimes, in summer, jack mackerel and bonito make a showing in the bay. Occasionally,
salmon are taken when a good run develops.

Within Monterey Bay, from early spring to late summer,
boat anglers troll for chinook salmon. Pacific sanddabs are
plentiful over sandy bottom, and California halibut are taken
trolling just beyond the surf line during summer and fall.

Anglers out of Moss Landing on Elkhorn Slough fish both
the tidewater section of the slough and outside in Monterey
Bay. The area around the entrance is particularly good for
Pacific Sanddab, sablefish, white croaker, and occasionally
California halibut. Salmon trolling is very popular with
Moss Landing anglers, who actively fish in the bay for chi-

nook salmon during the season(June and July are considered best). Surfperches are particularly abundant inside the slough. Jacksmelt, sand sole, staghorn sculpin, starry flounder, sharks and rays are also common in the estuary.

To the north and west, anglers who fish off Capitola bring in a mixed catch of blue rockfish, white croaker, Pacific sanddab, jacksmelt, and California halibut. Boats also work the area off the Seacliff pier and to the south for California halibut, starry flounder, white croaker, petrale sole, and sablefish. To the west, Santa Cruz small-boat anglers fish mainly the reef and kelp areas for rock-fishes(blue, grass and brown), lingcod and cabezon or troll along the sandy beaches to the east for halibut in summer. During the salmon season boats work the area between Sunset Beach and Davenport.

San Francisco Area Coast

Most offshore recreational fishing is for chinook sal-mon from spring through fall, although bottomfish tend to dominate the sport catch in areas south of San Pedro Point where salmon runs occur less predictably. In most years, migrating albacore are taken around the Farallon Islands in fall.

The main angling activities from Pigeon Point to Bean Hollow State Park is rock fishing. From Bean Hollow State Park north to Pillar Point the shore is alternately sandy beach and rocky outcroppings. Along this coast, striped bass begin to enter the shore angler's catch during summer and early fall; some of the better locations are Pescadero State Beach, San Gregorio State Beach, Martins Beach, and Half Moon Bay State Beaches. These are also good areas for surfperches.

Pillar Point Harbor on Half Moon Bay is the major re-creational fishing port along this section of coast, and party boats based at the harbor fish over nearshore and off-shore reefs for lingcod, cabezon, and rockfishes(blue, cop-per, olive and yellowtail). Occasional bottomfish trips are made to the Farallon Islands, and albacore are sometimes taken west of the Farallons from August to October. Small-

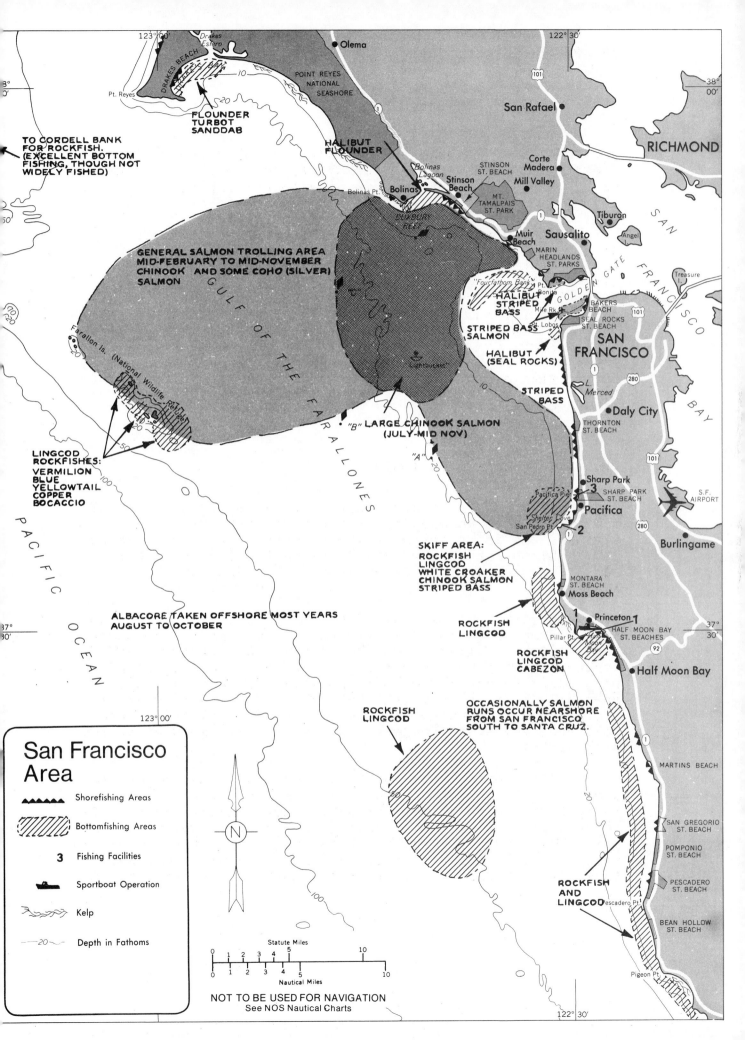

San Francisco Area

123° 00'

FLOUNDER
TURBOT
SANDDAB

• Olema

POINT REYES
NATIONAL
SEASHORE

122° 30'

38° 00'

101

• San Rafael

RICHMOND

Drakes
Estero

DRAKES BEACH

Pt. Reyes

10

20

TO CORDELL BANK
FOR ROCKFISH.
(EXCELLENT BOTTOM
FISHING, THOUGH NOT
WIDELY FISHED)

HALIBUT
FLOUNDER

Bolinas
Lagoon

Bolinas Pt.

Bolinas

STINSON
ST. BEACH

Stinson
Beach

Corte
Madera

Mill Valley

MT.
TAMALPAIS
ST. PARK

Tiburon

SAN

Angel

GENERAL SALMON TROLLING AREA
MID-FEBRUARY TO MID-NOVEMBER
CHINOOK   AND SOME COHO (SILVER)
SALMON

DUXBURY
REEF

Muir
Beach

MARIN
HEADLANDS
ST. PARKS

Sausalito

GOLDEN GATE

FRANCISCO

Treasure
I.

GULF OF THE

"Fourfathom Bank"

Pt.
Bonita

Mile Rk.

Lobos

BAKERS
BEACH

SEAL ROCKS
ST. BEACH

101

SAN
FRANCISCO

Farallon Is. (National Wildlife Refuge)

10

20

50

100

FARALLONES

HALIBUT
STRIPED
BASS

STRIPED BASS
SALMON

HALIBUT
(SEAL ROCKS)

STRIPED
BASS

L.
Merced

280

• Daly City

LINGCOD
ROCKFISHES:
VERMILION
BLUE
YELLOWTAIL
COPPER
BOCACCIO

Lightbucket

"B" LARGE CHINOOK SALMON
(JULY–MID NOV)

"A"

20

THORNTON
ST. BEACH

S.F.
AIRPORT

• Sharp Park

3

SHARP PARK
ST. BEACH

280

PACIFIC

Pacifica Pier

Shelter Cove

San Pedro Pt.

Pacifica

2

• Burlingame

101

ALBACORE TAKEN OFFSHORE MOST YEARS
AUGUST TO OCTOBER

37° 30'

SKIFF AREA:
ROCKFISH
LINGCOD
WHITE CROAKER
CHINOOK SALMON
STRIPED BASS

MONTARA
ST. BEACH

Moss Beach

ROCKFISH
LINGCOD

1

• Princeton

1

Pillar Pt.

HALF MOON BAY
ST. BEACHES

37° 30'

92

ROCKFISH
LINGCOD
CABEZON

• Half Moon Bay

OCEAN

ROCKFISH
LINGCOD

OCCASIONALLY SALMON
RUNS OCCUR NEARSHORE
FROM SAN FRANCISCO
SOUTH TO SANTA CRUZ.

50

20

MARTINS BEACH

1

SAN GREGORIO
ST. BEACH

POMPONIO
ST. BEACH

PESCADERO
ST. BEACH

123° 00'

San Francisco
Area

▲▲▲ Shorefishing Areas

//// Bottomfishing Areas

3 Fishing Facilities

🚤 Sportboat Operation

〰 Kelp

— 20 — Depth in Fathoms

N

ROCKFISH
AND
LINGCOD

Pescadero Pt.

BEAN HOLLOW
ST. BEACH

100

Statute Miles

0 1 2 3 4 5   10

0 1 2 3 4 5   10

Nautical Miles

NOT TO BE USED FOR NAVIGATION
See NOS Nautical Charts

Pigeon Pt.

122° 30'

boat anglers actively fish for salmon when the fish make a showing nearshore, or fish on the bottom around the entrance to the harbor and north along Pillar Point for rockfishes (blue, black, canary, copper, and olive), lingcod, cabezon, and white croaker.

North of Pillar Point the coast becomes rocky once again until you reach Montara State Beach - a narrow, coarse-sand beach backed by sandstone bluffs. Here surf casters take surfperches and catch striped bass during the summer.

From the public fishing pier at Pacifica north to the Golden Gate, the coast is mostly sandy beach, and it is along these beaches that the heaviest runs of striped bass occur in the surf. The map shows some of the more popular fishing spots, although this entire coast is good for striped bass when they are running. One of the most heavily fished places is Bakers Beach near the Golden Gate Bridge. These ocean beaches are also good bait-casting areas for surfperch during winter and spring.

The Gulf of the Farallons is fished primarily by San Francisco Bay boats and occasionally boats from Half Moon Bay. This area produces the most consistent ocean sport fishing for salmon in the state. Most fishing is for chinook salmon, although some coho also are landed. The season extends from mid-February through mid-November(check state regulations), and there are two major chinook runs - one in the spring and one in the fall. During the height of the spring run from about March to June, most fishing occurs offshore between Duxbury Reef and the Farallon Islands, while from July to mid-October the fish are taken closer to shore. The most productive area for large fall-run chinook extends from the San Francisco light buoy, or "light bucket," former site of the San Francisco lightship, to the Marin County beaches and north to Duxbury Reef, where fishing is best from July through September. The Golden Gate area, especially around Mile Rock and the south tower of the bridge, is also a good fishing stop in midsummer and fall for striped bass and occasionally salmon.

When salmon are not running, boats may fish for rock-fishes(yellowtail, bocaccio, copper, blue, and vermilion), and lingcod around the Farallon Islands, and occasionally travel as far west as Cordell Bank, about 20 miles west of Point Reyes.

There is some fishing for chinook salmon off Muir and Stinson Beaches in late summer, but weather and sea often restrict small-boat fishing in the ocean. Fourfathom Bank (also called Potato Patch Shoal) can get particularly rough on windy days, but in calm weather this sandy shoal area is a good fishing spot for California halibut and striped bass. California halibut are also taken around Seal Rocks and to the south(July and August are best).

Pt Reyes to Ft Ross Coast

Along this rural and often wind-swept part of the coast boats operate year-round, weather permitting, out of Bodega Harbor and Dillon Beach. Most offshore fishing is for bottomfish - particularly rockfishes or "rock cod." Some boats also fish for chinook salmon when the fish are running, but, in general, salmon appear less predictably here than off San Francisco and areas to the north.

The range of the fleet extends south to off Point Reyes and north to Fort Ross. Areas most frequented by boaters are Tomales Point, the 27-fathom reefs off the western shore of Point Reyes Peninsula, and areas north along the coast from Bodega Head to Fort Ross. Occasionally, trips are made to Cordell Bank, about 23 miles southwest of the Bodega Harbor entrance. Most of the boat catch is made up of rockfishes (yellowtail, blue, yelloweye or turkey-red, chilipepper, bocaccio, canary, black, and copper). Other rocky-bottom fishes such as cabezon and lingcod are also caught along with an occasional chinook. Lingcod appear to be more plentiful in the northern areas off Fort Ross than in areas to the south, and flatfish are sometimes taken incidentally as boats drift from rocky to sandy bottom.

In Tomales Bay, the salmon season is open all year, but fishing for chinook is often erratic even at the peak of the season(July, August, and September). Coho make a modest showing around October and November.

Small-boat fishing is generally limited to the confines of Tomales Bay and around the entrance to Bodega Harbor. Inside Tomales Bay, small-boat anglers fish for sharks and rays, California halibut(June to October), sand sole, turbot, jack-

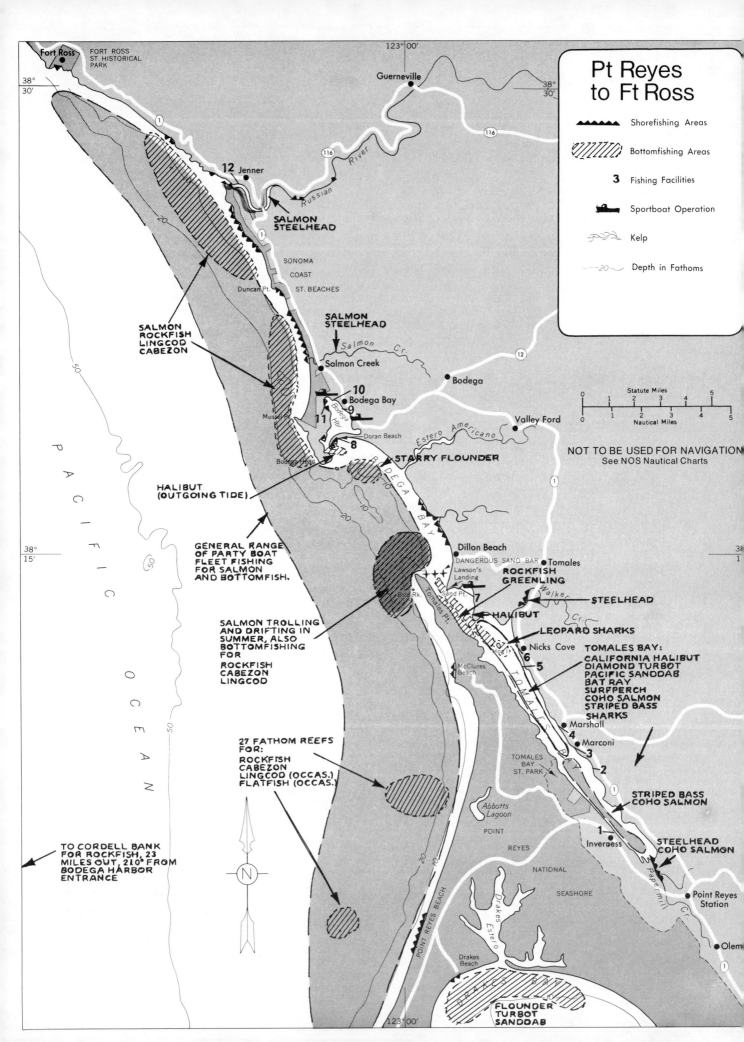

Pt Reyes to Ft Ross

▲▲▲	Shorefishing Areas
▨	Bottomfishing Areas
3	Fishing Facilities
🚤	Sportboat Operation
〰	Kelp
—20—	Depth in Fathoms

Fort Ross

FORT ROSS ST. HISTORICAL PARK

38° 30'

123° 00'

Guerneville

Russian River

116

12 Jenner

SALMON STEELHEAD

SONOMA COAST ST. BEACHES

Duncan Pt.

20

SALMON ROCKFISH LINGCOD CABEZON

50

SALMON STEELHEAD

Salmon Cr.

12

Salmon Creek

Bodega

Mussel Pt.

10
9 Bodega Bay

11

Bodega Hbr.

Doran Beach

Estero Americano

Valley Ford

8

Bodega Head

STARRY FLOUNDER

BODEGA BAY

38° 30'
1

HALIBUT (OUTGOING TIDE)

PACIFIC OCEAN

GENERAL RANGE OF PARTY BOAT FLEET FISHING FOR SALMON AND BOTTOMFISH.

38° 15'

50

Dillon Beach

DANGEROUS SAND BAR

Lawson's Landing

Tomales

ROCKFISH GREENLING

Walker Cr.

STEELHEAD

20

10

Sand Pt.

7

Tomales Pt.

HALIBUT

LEOPARD SHARKS

SALMON TROLLING AND DRIFTING IN SUMMER, ALSO BOTTOMFISHING FOR ROCKFISH CABEZON LINGCOD

Nicks Cove

6

5

TOMALES BAY: CALIFORNIA HALIBUT DIAMOND TURBOT PACIFIC SANDDAB BAT RAY SURFPERCH COHO SALMON STRIPED BASS SHARKS

McClures Beach

TOMALES BAY

4 Marshall

3 Marconi

TOMALES BAY ST. PARK

2

27 FATHOM REEFS FOR: ROCKFISH CABEZON LINGCOD (OCCAS.) FLATFISH (OCCAS.)

Abbotts Lagoon

POINT

REYES

STRIPED BASS COHO SALMON

1

Inverness

STEELHEAD COHO SALMON

NATIONAL

SEASHORE

Papermill Cr.

Point Reyes Station

TO CORDELL BANK FOR ROCKFISH, 23 MILES OUT, 210° FROM BODEGA HARBOR ENTRANCE

N

POINT REYES BEACH

20

10

Drakes Estero

Drakes Beach

FLOUNDER TURBOT SANDDAB

Olema

1

NOT TO BE USED FOR NAVIGATION
See NOS Nautical Charts

Statute Miles
0 1 2 3 4 5
0 1 2 3 4 5
Nautical Miles

123° 00'

smelt(September to November is best), and an assortment of surfperches. Sharks are particularly plentiful in the bay. Striped bass sometimes are caught in the southern reaches of the bay in summer. The lower bay also has a small run of coho salmon which are caught trolling during October and November, and some steelhead are taken as they make their way to Papermill Creek to spawn(November to February).

In Bodega Harbor, a narrow channel cuts through this shallow lagoon to the boat basin at the town of Bodega Bay and into deeper water at the harbor's northwest corner. There is a limited amount of fishing for surfperches and starry flounder in deepwater parts of the lagoon, and steelhead occasionally are taken around areas of freshwater seepage.

Selected areas of this coast offer many different types of shore fishing, including casting along sandy beaches for surfperches, pier and dock fishing in bays and harbors. Spring and early summer are best for surfperches, coho salmon appear in the fall from September to November, and most rocky-shore fishes are taken year-round.

The sandy beaches along the Point Reyes Peninsula provide good fishing for surfperches. Most of the peninsula is within the boundaries of the Point Reyes National Seashore.

Along the Tomales Bay shore, pier and dock fishing is available at some of the small-boat harbors and wharves. Jacksmelt and surfperches are the most common pier-caught species. At the very southern end of the bay, coho salmon are taken near the entrance of Papermill Creek(October to November). On the eastern shore, near the entrance to Tomales Bay, surfperches are taken by shore casting along beaches north of Sand Point, and fishing is excellent for rockfish and greenlings where the sandy beach gives way to a predominantly rocky coastline north of Dillon Beach.

The next opportunity for shore fishing as you approach Bodega Bay from the south is found at Doran Beach Park. Most fishing takes place around the east jetty at the mouth of the harbor where the usual fare is surfperches, jacksmelt, starry flounder, rockfishes, and greenlings. Anglers also fish from the west jetty on the other side of the harbor entrance for the same species.

In the town of Bodega Bay the public is allowed to
fish from the local wharf where the main species taken are
jacksmelt, young bocaccio and surfperches. There is some
fishing along the breakwater on the western shore of Bodega
Harbor for surfperches and black rockfishes.

On beaches along the Sonoma coast, anglers catch surfperches, lingcod, rockfishes and flounder.

Ft Ross to Cape Mendocino Coast

From Fort Ross to Cape Mandocino the shoreline is predominantly rocky backed by high grassy bluffs. These rugged
headlands are sharply indented with numerous gulches, and
public access to shore occurs infrequently because of the
steep terrain and the many privately owned areas adjacent
to the coast. Most shore fishing occurs at coves and beaches
where coastal streams and rivers empty into the sea. Winters
are wet and chilly, and in summer the coast is usually fog-
bound. Fall is the sunniest and most pleasant time of year.

Most ocean sport fishing takes place out of the town of
Fort Bragg and to a lesser extent at Albion, Point Arena and
Shelter Cove. Bottomfishing along this rocky coast is ex-
cellent, and salmon trolling is very popular.

Where the shore can be reached, rock anglers seek lingcod, cabezon, and small rockfishes and where rocky shores are
interrupted by stretches of sandy beach, surf casters fish
for surfperch during spring and summer(April and May are considered best).

Sport fishing boats operate out of Noyo Harbor, in Fort
Bragg, and in some years out of Albion when weather permits.
Most fishing is during the summer. The rocky reefs along
this coast are extremely productive for lingcod, cabezon,
kelp greenling, and rockfishes(blue, black, yellowtail, olive,
copper, canary, yelloweye, vermillion and chilipepper). Reef
areas around rocky points adjacent to the Noyo and Albion
river mouths are excellent spots for lingcod and red rockfish.

Offshore anglers troll for chinook and coho salmon from

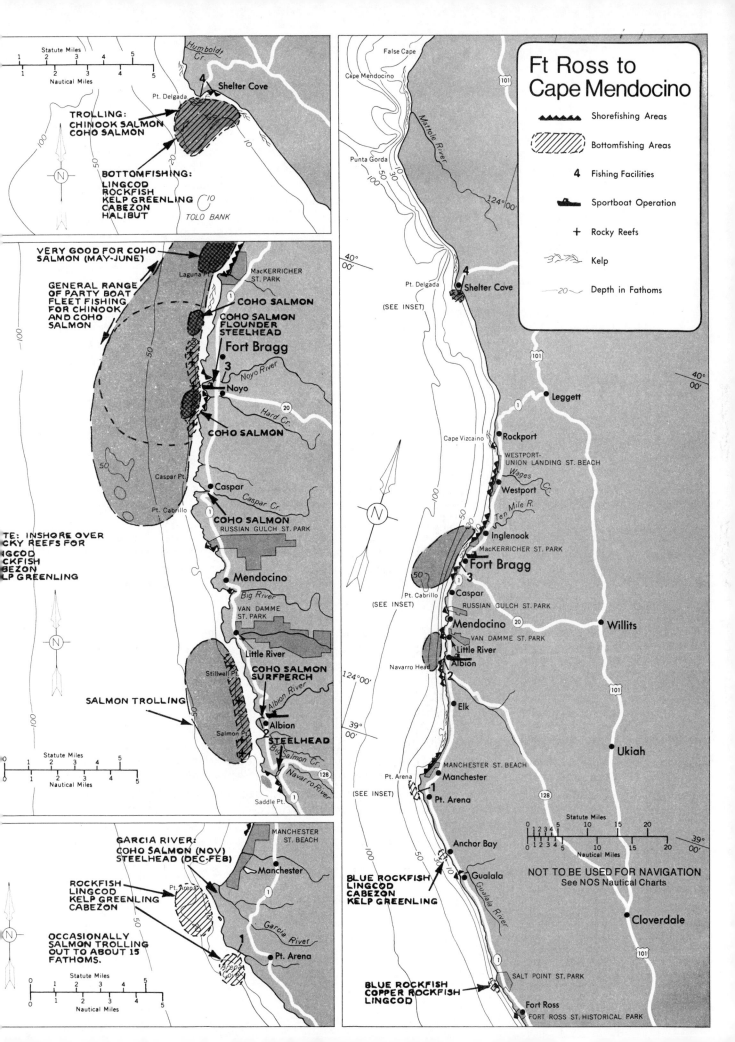

Ft Ross to Cape Mendocino

▲▲▲▲▲	Shorefishing Areas
▨	Bottomfishing Areas
4	Fishing Facilities
⛵	Sportboat Operation
+	Rocky Reefs
〜	Kelp
—20—	Depth in Fathoms

Inset (top left):

Statute Miles
1 2 3 4 5
Nautical Miles
1 2 3 4 5

TROLLING:
CHINOOK SALMON
COHO SALMON

BOTTOMFISHING:
LINGCOD
ROCKFISH
KELP GREENLING
CABEZON
HALIBUT

Humboldt Cr.
Pt. Delgada
Shelter Cove
TOLO BANK

Middle left inset:

VERY GOOD FOR COHO SALMON (MAY-JUNE)

GENERAL RANGE OF PARTY BOAT FLEET FISHING FOR CHINOOK AND COHO SALMON

Laguna Pt.
MacKERRICHER ST. PARK
COHO SALMON
COHO SALMON
FLOUNDER
STEELHEAD
Fort Bragg
3
Noyo
Noyo River
Hard Cr.
COHO SALMON

NOTE: INSHORE OVER ROCKY REEFS FOR
LINGCOD
ROCKFISH
CABEZON
KELP GREENLING

Caspar Pt.
Caspar
Pt. Cabrillo
COHO SALMON
RUSSIAN GULCH ST. PARK
Mendocino
Big River
VAN DAMME ST. PARK
Little River
COHO SALMON
SURFPERCH
SALMON TROLLING
Stillwell Pt.
Salmon Pt.
Albion
Albion River
STEELHEAD
Big Salmon Cr.
Navarro River
Saddle Pt.

Statute Miles
1 2 3 4 5
Nautical Miles
1 2 3 4 5

Bottom left inset:

GARCIA RIVER:
COHO SALMON (NOV)
STEELHEAD (DEC-FEB)

ROCKFISH
LINGCOD
KELP GREENLING
CABEZON

OCCASIONALLY SALMON TROLLING OUT TO ABOUT 15 FATHOMS.

MANCHESTER ST. BEACH
Manchester
Pt. Arena
1
Garcia River
Pt. Arena
Arena Cove

Statute Miles
1 2 3 4 5
Nautical Miles
1 2 3 4 5

Main map (right):

False Cape
Cape Mendocino
101
Mattole River
Punta Gorda
124° 00'
40° 00'
Pt. Delgada
4
Shelter Cove
(SEE INSET)
101
Leggett
1
Cape Vizcaino
Rockport
WESTPORT-UNION LANDING ST. BEACH
Wages
Westport
Ten Mile R.
Inglenook
MacKERRICHER ST. PARK
Fort Bragg
1 3
Pt. Cabrillo
(SEE INSET)
Caspar
RUSSIAN GULCH ST. PARK
Mendocino
20
Willits
VAN DAMME ST. PARK
Little River
Navarro Head
Albion
2
Elk
124° 00'
39° 00'
101
Ukiah
MANCHESTER ST. BEACH
Manchester
Pt. Arena
(SEE INSET)
1
Pt. Arena
128

Statute Miles
1 2 3 4 5 10 15 20
Nautical Miles
1 2 3 4 5 10 15 20

40° 00'

39° 00'

Anchor Bay
BLUE ROCKFISH
LINGCOD
CABEZON
KELP GREENLING
Gualala
Gualala River

NOT TO BE USED FOR NAVIGATION
See NOS Nautical Charts

Cloverdale

BLUE ROCKFISH
COPPER ROCKFISH
LINGCOD
SALT POINT ST. PARK
Fort Ross
FORT ROSS ST. HISTORICAL PARK

1

May to October in water 10-60 fathoms deep. At the height
of the season in July and August, coho move inshore to feed
over reef areas, and during October and November they congregate around river and creek mouths such as the Ten Mile
River, Noyo River, Albion River, Caspar Creek, and the Navarro River. During this time fishing reaches its peak around
the Noyo River mouth. Most ocean fishing(for both salmon
and bottomfish) occurs within 3 miles of the whistle buoy
about a mile west of the mouth of the Noyo River.

Shore anglers looking for spots to fish on the coast
around the Fort Bragg-Albion area can try their luck between
the towns of Elk and Albion, and at the State Parks. Most
of these areas have good rock fishing and beaches are good
for surfperches.

Eel River to Oregon Coast

North of Cape Mendocino, dark sand beaches begin to
interrupt rocky headlands more frequently, and large rivers,
famous for their migrating salmon and sea-run trout, empty
into the sea. The terrain is less steep near the ocean than
areas to the south, but the coastline still maintains a rugged beauty of its own. Along this coast the magnificent
coastal redwood trees thrive in the cool and very damp cli-
mate so typical of the Pacific Northwest.

Salmon is by far the most important game fish in this
region, and both chinook and coho salmon are taken during
summer and fall. Rockfishes and other bottomfishes also
enter the sport catch, especially in the north, but this
type of fishing usually runs a distant second to salmon
fishing.

Surfperch are abundant and are available year-round
along sandy beaches and in tidewater, with spring and early
summer bringing the best catches. Along the occasional
rocky stretches, black and grass rockfishes, and kelp and
rock greenlings are taken by rock anglers. In most places
there is year-round fishing in tidewater for starry flounder and surfperches, with spring bringing the best catches.

North of the Eel River U.S. 101 turns toward the coast as

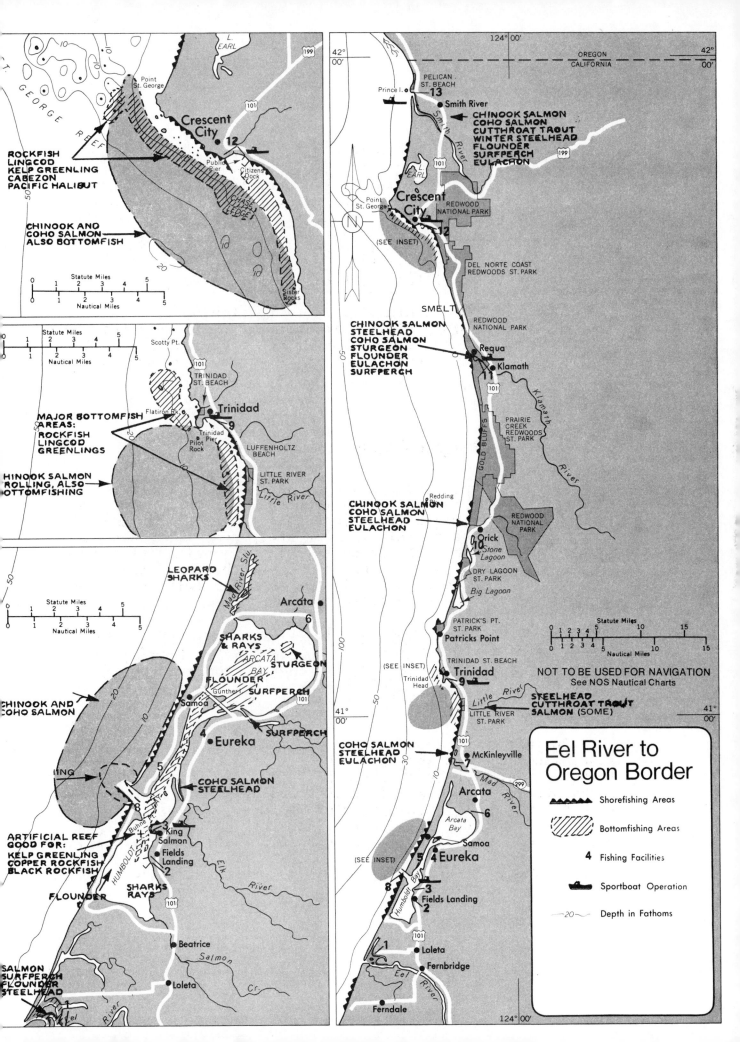

Eel River to Oregon Border

Inset map (upper left) — Crescent City area:

ROCKFISH
LINGCOD
KELP GREENLING
CABEZON
PACIFIC HALIBUT

CHINOOK AND
COHO SALMON
ALSO BOTTOMFISH

Point St. George
Crescent City 12
Public Pier
Citizens Dock
CHART LEDGE
Sister Rocks
KELP REEF
ST GEORGE REEF
L. EARL
199
101

Statute Miles
0 1 2 3 4 5
Nautical Miles
0 1 2 3 4 5

Inset map (middle left) — Trinidad area:

MAJOR BOTTOMFISH
AREAS:
ROCKFISH
LINGCOD
GREENLINGS

CHINOOK SALMON
TROLLING, ALSO
BOTTOMFISHING

Scotty Pt.
TRINIDAD ST. BEACH
Trinidad 9
Flatiron Rk.
Trinidad Pier
Pilot Rock
LUFFENHOLTZ BEACH
LITTLE RIVER ST. PARK
Little River
101

Statute Miles
0 1 2 3 4 5
Nautical Miles
0 1 2 3 4 5

Inset map (lower left) — Eureka / Humboldt Bay area:

LEOPARD SHARKS

SHARKS & RAYS
ARCATA BAY
STURGEON
FLOUNDER
SURFPERCH

CHINOOK AND
COHO SALMON

SURFPERCH

COHO SALMON
STEELHEAD

ARTIFICIAL REEF
GOOD FOR:
KELP GREENLING
COPPER ROCKFISH
BLACK ROCKFISH

FLOUNDER

SHARKS
RAYS

SALMON
SURFPERCH
FLOUNDER
STEELHEAD

Mad River Slu.
Arcata 6
Samoa
Gunther I.
Eureka 4
Buhne Pt.
HUMBOLDT BAY
King Salmon
Fields Landing 2
Elk River
Beatrice
Loleta
Salmon Cr.
Eel River
101

Statute Miles
0 1 2 3 4 5
Nautical Miles
0 1 2 3 4 5

Main map (right) — Eel River to Oregon Border:

OREGON
CALIFORNIA
124° 00'
42° 00'   42° 00'

PELICAN ST. BEACH
Prince I. 13
Smith River

CHINOOK SALMON
COHO SALMON
CUTTHROAT TROUT
WINTER STEELHEAD
FLOUNDER
SURFPERCH
EULACHON

L. EARL
Point St. George
Crescent City 12
REDWOOD NATIONAL PARK
(SEE INSET)
DEL NORTE COAST REDWOODS ST. PARK
Smith River
199
101

SMELT

CHINOOK SALMON
STEELHEAD
COHO SALMON
STURGEON
FLOUNDER
EULACHON
SURFPERCH

REDWOOD NATIONAL PARK
Requa
Klamath 11
GOLD BLUFFS
PRAIRIE CREEK REDWOODS ST. PARK
Klamath River
101

CHINOOK SALMON
COHO SALMON
STEELHEAD
EULACHON

Redding
Orick 10
Stone Lagoon
DRY LAGOON ST. PARK
Big Lagoon
REDWOOD NATIONAL PARK

PATRICK'S PT. ST. PARK
Patricks Point
TRINIDAD ST. BEACH
(SEE INSET)
Trinidad 9
Trinidad Head
Little River
LITTLE RIVER ST. PARK

STEELHEAD
CUTTHROAT TROUT
SALMON (SOME)

NOT TO BE USED FOR NAVIGATION
See NOS Nautical Charts

41° 00'   41° 00'

COHO SALMON
STEELHEAD
EULACHON

McKinleyville 7
Arcata 6
Mad River
Arcata Bay
Samoa
Eureka 4 5
(SEE INSET)
Humboldt Bay
Fields Landing 2 3
8
Loleta 1
Fernbridge
Eel River
Ferndale
101
299

Statute Miles
0 1 2 3 4 5   10   15
Nautical Miles
0 1 2 3 4 5   10   15

124° 00'

Legend:

Shorefishing Areas

Bottomfishing Areas

4 — Fishing Facilities

Sportboat Operation

—20— Depth in Fathoms

it approaches the town of Eureka, a center of fishing activity during the salmon season. A sizeable party boat and boat fishery operates out of Humboldt Bay, and boats fish almost exclusively for chinook and coho. Standard fishing methods are trolling and drifting("mooching") bait close to the bottom. Fishing takes place from May to October with chinook being the first to show. July and August are considered the best fishing months as significant numbers of coho begin to be caught. Salmon move in close to the beaches and around the jetties at the harbor entrance as the season progresses. During this time sport boats venture out into the ocean to join the party boat fleet and the entrance channel soon becomes a favorite spot for chinook fishing.

Inside Humboldt Bay there is tidewater fishing from boats for jacksmelt, sharks, rays and surfperches. Sharks are plentiful in Arcata Bay and leopard shark fishing is excellent in Mad River Slough during summer. Sturgeons sometimes are taken around the ruins of the old lumber loading ramp at the head of Arcata Channel. South Humboldt Bay is mostly a clamming area, but there also is angling for some of the species mentioned above and rockfishes which are consistently taken by anglers over the artificial reef during the slack tide and when the water is clear. Rockfishes are taken also around the breakwater at Buhne Point.

The ocean beaches adjacent to the Humboldt Bay entrance from the North and South spits have shore fishing. On the South Spit, anglers cast for surfperches. The south jetty is a popular fishing spot for blue and black rockfishes, kelp greenling, lingcod, cabezon, surfperches, jacksmelt, and coho and chinook salmon(in summer). Species caught from the North Spit are similar to those taken along the South Spit. Another jetty, on the bay side of the North Spit, is a good spot for lingcod, kelp greenling, cabezon, and rockfishes(blue, black and grass).

Trinidad Harbor offers ocean salmon fishing and bottom-fishing in summer, and pier and rocky-shore fishing year-round. The salmon catch is mostly coho, and best fishing is in July and August. Blue and black rockfishes, lingcod, kelp greenling, and cabezon are caught in the salmon fishing areas and inshore over rocky reefs. There is pier fishing in the harbor for jacksmelt, surfperches, kelp greenling and cabezon.

To the north, rockfishes, greenlings and surfperches are taken from rocky beaches at Trinidad State Beach and Patricks Point State Park.

The harbor at Crescent City is well protected from sea and weather by extensive seawalls which flank its perimeter and by the Point St. George headland. The fishing fleet is based at Crescent City Boat Basin between the east seawall and the public fishing pier, an area known as Citizen's Dock. Party boat and boat anglers fish for salmon and bottomfish, weather permitting. Salmon trolling(mainly for chinook) usually begins in June and continues through September, with best catches made in July and August. Lingcod, cabezon, kelp greenling, rockfishes, and Pacific halibut also are taken in the salmon areas, but best bottomfishing is found usually farther inshore close to rocky reefs along the 5-fathom curve from Sister Rocks to the harbor entrance and along the 10-fathom curve from Chase Ledge north to St. George's Reef. Species of rockfish that enter the catch include black, blue, china, vermilion, and bocaccio.

Shore anglers take blue and black rockfishes, lingcod, and kelp and rock greenlings form the west breakwater and along rocky shores north to Point St. George. There is pier fishing at Citizen's Dock for starry flounder, kelp greenling, surfperches and jacksmelt.

The Bays

San Francisco Bay, California's largest estuary, techni-
cally is divided into three connecting bays - San Francisco
Bay proper, San Pablo Bay, and Suisun Bay. These bays receive
large volumes of freshwater runoff from the extensive Sacramento and San Joaquin River systems that drain California's
Central Valley and have their source in the Sierra Nevada. In
general, most of the San Francisco Bay system is very shallow
(the average depth is 20 feet) and there are extensive mudflats
in San Pablo Bay and south San Francisco Bay.

The two most sought-after game fishes in the San Francisco Bay area are the striped bass and chinook salmon. Most
salmon fishing takes place in the ocean outside the Golden
Gate, while San Francisco Bay is practically the unrivaled
domain of the striped bass angler. Other fishes such as
sturgeon, starry flounder, surfperches, jacksmelt, topsmelt,
white croaker, rockfishes, sharks, and rays also offer a great
deal of sport to Bay area anglers.

San Francisco, San Pablo and Suisun Bays provide a wonderful year-round fishery. The keys to successful fishing in
these bays, beyond using the right techniques, is to fish in
the right place and to fish at the right times(see Fishing
Tips below).

Fishing Seasons   (+=good, -=fair)

Species	J	F	M	A	M	J	J	A	S	O	N	D
Striper		-	-	-	-	-	-	+	+	+	+	-
Halibut						+	+	+	-			
Sturgeon	+*	+*	+*	-	-	-	-	-	-	--	+	+
Salmon								-	-	-		

*closure in some Bay waters

Fishing Tips

Fishing during the prime tidal movements is extremely
important. The best time to fish these Bays is during the
two-week cycle of extreme water movement that is a result of
the maximum difference between high and low tide. More rapidly moving waters move bait and this produces more active
feeding for all game fish in the Bays. Concentrate fishing

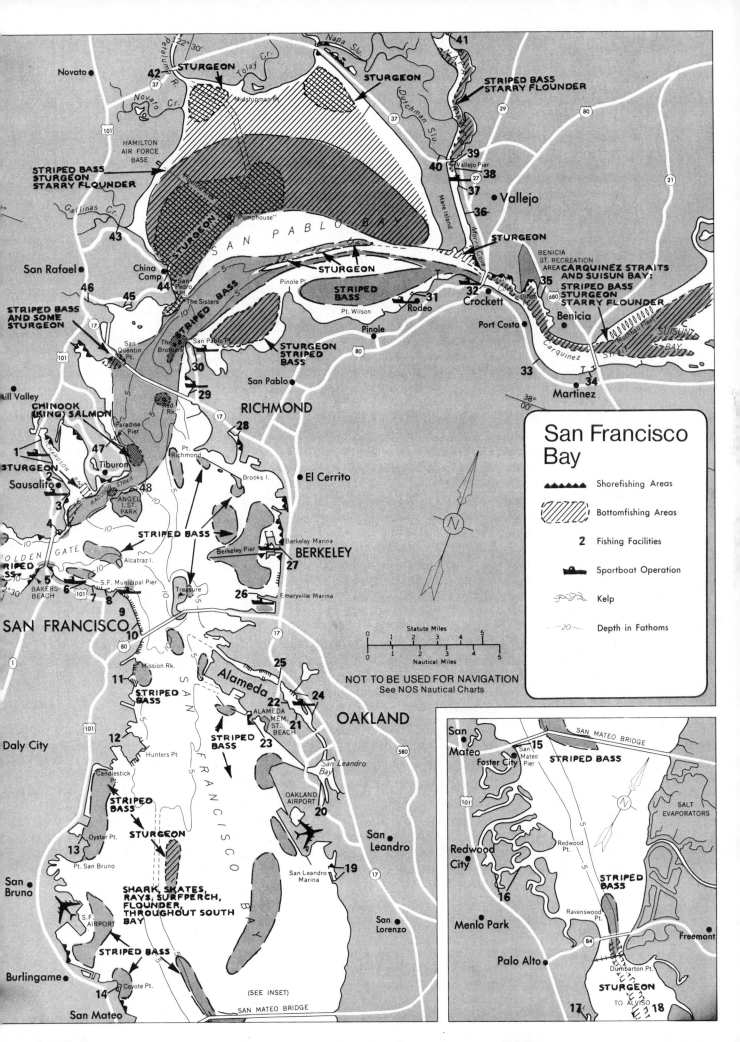

from the 2-3 hours before the high water slack period until an hour or two after the ebb starts. This will produce the best results. This period is even more productive if it occurs at first light or dusk.

Striped Bass

Striped bass spawn from about April to mid-June in fresh waters of the Sacramento and San Joaquin rivers. After spawning, the fish move back down into the saltwater bays; some venture out into the ocean. They spend most of the summer and fall in salt water before returning once again to brackish-water and freshwater sloughs and rivers. Although best fishing times vary with area, in general, the fishing season extends from March to December, with best fishing from mid-August to November. October has been the best striped bass fishing month consistently since 1969.

In San Pablo Bay, Carquinez Strait, and Suisun Bay, striped bass are caught year-round with best fishing usually in October and November, with a lesser run of fish in June, July and August. Most spring and summer fish are caught trolling in the late afternoon. Fall-run fish are caught still fishing or drifting, primarily with live bait such as staghorn sculpin(known locally as "bullheads").

In the Napa River and nearby brackish-water sloughs along the northern shore of San Pablo Bay, striped bass are caught throughout the year although weather sometimes restricts fishing during the winter months. Best times are considered to be September, October, and November, peaking usually in late October. Fish are taken by bait fishing and trolling from boats and bait casting from shore.

Within San Francisco Bay proper, in such areas as the Golden Gate Bridge(south tower), Raccoon Strait(over Raccoon Shoal), Berkeley flats, and off Alcatraz and Treasure Islands, fishing usually starts in June and extends through October into November. Most fish are caught after mid-August, with peak catches in October. A popular fishing method is drifting with live bait(anchovies or shiner surfperch) in areas where an abrupt change in depth occurs and when the current is running swiftest. Anglers also troll for stripers, and some will even get out their plug casting gear when a surface-feeding school is located. From Angel Island north to The Brothers, good striped bass fishing can usually be had in Sep-

tember, October, and November by drifting live bait and trolling as fish migrate through on their way back to the Sacramen-
to/San Joaquin Delta.

Shore and pier fishermen cast lures and bait for stripers
from selected spots on both sides of the Bay. Shore fishing
at night for striped bass is legal in the Bay.

The striped bass season in south San Francisco Bay extends
from June through September, and in some years fishing may last
until November or December. Fishing usually reaches a peak
around the San Mateo Bridge area in June and July and around
the Dumbarton Bridge in September and October. Most striper
fishing in south San Francisco Bay is a trolling affair with
some plug casting when a school is found. Also, a growing
number of anglers are fly fishing from shore for striped bass
in spring and again in late summer around San Francisco Airport
and Coyote Point.

Sturgeon

Sturgeon fishing has become very popular in the Bay Area
over the years, especially in San Pablo Bay, Carquinez Strait
and Suisun Bay. A small but growing sturgeon fishery is also
developing in south San Francisco Bay from off Oyster Point
(San Bruno Shoals) south to the entrance of Alviso Slough.
Both green and white sturgeons are taken; the white sturgeon
is the most prized.

Although sturgeons are caught throughout the year in the
upper bays, best fishing is usually in the fall and winter
when the biggest fish are taken. In San Pablo Bay, they appear to move in over the flats in early fall, and fishing usually lasts from November to May, with the best catches being
from about January to March. The flats along the north side
of the bay from the Mare Island jetty("Rockwall") to China
Camp are especially productive at high tide during the winter.
Other good spots in San Pablo Bay are the "pump house" and
around the odd-numbered buoys that mark the north side of the
main channel which cuts through the middle of the bay. There
is also year-round fishing in Carquinez Strait over the flats
along the northern shore. Smaller fish taken are in summer,
larger ones in winter.

In Suisun Bay, fishing usually starts in spring around April and lasts until October or November, about the time of the first rains. In summer, most Suisun sturgeon are sub-legal size(less than 40 inches long) with about 1 "keeper" out of every 10 caught. Larger fish are taken in the fall. The "mothball fleet" and the channel buoys along the edges on sand bars near the entrance to the bay are good areas to fish.

In south San Francisco Bay from San Bruno Shoals south to Alviso Slough, the season extends from about November to March. Early season fishing is usually best in the northerly areas; late season fishing is usually best in the more southerly areas along the edge of the channel.

Sometimes during the Pacific herring runs, which occur anytime between December and March, sturgeons are taken from boats and shore in the central part of the bay in such areas as Richardson Bay and along the Sausalito waterfront.

Halibut

In San Francisco Bay, some of the best places to fish for halibut are;

- Near Crissy Field

- Off western tip of Alcatraz Island

- Flats north and west of Treasure Island

- Raccoon Straits

- Between Golden Gate Field and Emeryville Marina

- Between Oyster Point and San Francisco International Airport

Other Bay Sport Fishes

Although most salmon are taken outside the Golden Gate, migrating chinook salmon sometimes are caught deep trolling with whole anchovies in the area from the Golden Gate to Raccoon Strait and off the Tiburon Peninsula north to the

Richmond Bridge during late summer. The area off the eastern
side of the Tiburon Peninsula(called "California City" by
anglers) is heavily fished when the salmon are running in
September and October.

Sharks, skates, and rays are plentiful throughout the
bay; some of the more common types are leopard, brown, smooth-
hound, and sevengill sharks, spiny dogfish, bat ray, and big
skate. These are especially numerous in south San Francisco
Bay all year. Most fishing, however, takes place in summer
and fall.

Starry flounder are abundant, especially over the flats
in San Pablo and Suisun Bays and in the Napa River and adjacent sloughs. Many are taken in these areas, and throughout
the bay system, by shore and boat anglers(winter and spring
are best).

An assortment of surfperches also are taken in San
Francisco Bay - mostly from piers and from shore. Spring
is considered the best season. Some of the more common
species are shiner, walleye, white, rubberlip, black, pile,
striped, and rainbow surfperches.

Other fish prevalent in the pier and shore catch include white croaker("kingfish"), staghorn sculpin("bullhead")
jacksmelt, topsmelt, English sole, sand sole, small lingcod,
and brown and black rockfishes.

208

The Delta

The Sacramento-San Joaquin Delta is a 1000 square mile area of diked islands, elevated levee roads and meandering, interlocking waterways where the Sacramento and San Joaquin rivers come together. There are over 1000 miles of navigable waterways. Fishing in these waterways and rivers is excellent. Striped bass(to 30-40 pounds) and sturgeon(to several hundred pounds) are the most prized catches. But the Delta also provides excellent black bass, catfish and panfish, as well as an occasional migrating salmon.

Fishing Seasons   (+=good, -=fair)

Species	J	F	M	A	M	J	J	A	S	O	N	D
Striper	+	+	+	-	-	-			-	-	+	+
Sturgeon	+	+	-	-	-	-	-	-	-	-	-	+
Salmon										-	-	-
Black Bass		-	+	+	-	-	-	-	+	+		
Catfish	-	-	-	-	-	-	-	-	-	-	-	-
Panfish	-	-	-	+	+	+	-	-	-	-	-	-

Fishing Tips

Stripers feed most actively on moving water, so it's best to fish when there is a big tide swing. When still fishing for stripers from a boat, fish right where a sandbar drops-off. Position your boat(anchored) on the upstream side of the bar on an incoming tide and on the downstream drop-off on an outgoing tide. If tide movements are modest, trolling might be a better option. Remember the striper, black bass and catfish are all bottomfeeders, so whether you're fishing with bait or trolling, make sure your offering is near the bottom. The locations marked for specific species are meant to highlight those specific sloughs that are consistently good producers. But, the sloughs and rivers in the Delta are miles and miles long. So, keep moving in a particular slough until you find fish. Also, the indicated locations are not the only places you can find fish. For example, catfish and stripers(especially in late winter-early spring) can be found in many places in the Delta. And any of the back sloughs will produce panfish.

The maps in this section are intended only to show choice fishing spots. See Hal Shell's Delta Map for facilities, launch ramps, and specific navigational information.

Northwest Delta

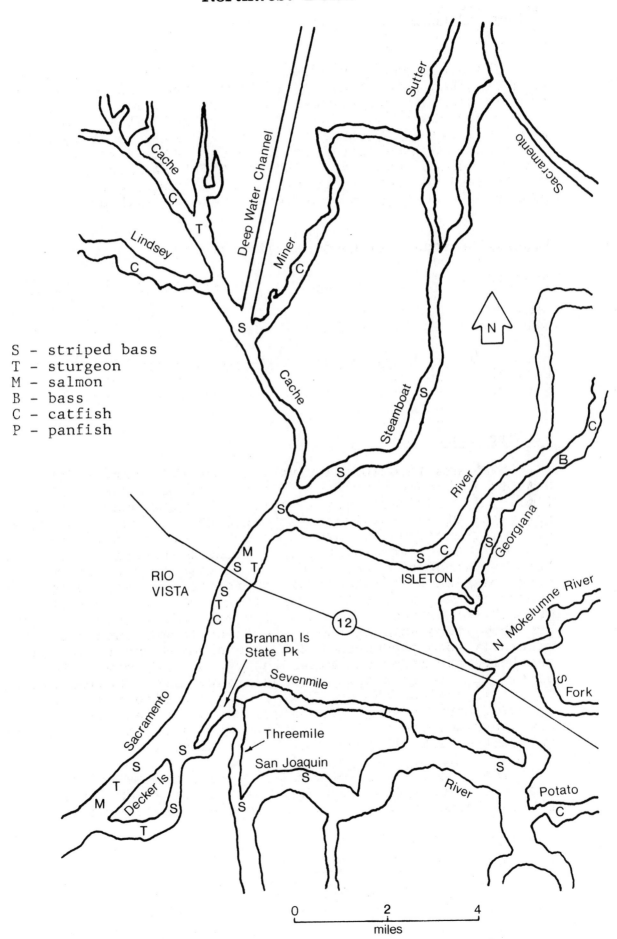

S – striped bass
T – sturgeon
M – salmon
B – bass
C – catfish
P – panfish

RIO
VISTA

ISLETON

Brannan Is
State Pk

Sevenmile

Threemile

San Joaquin

Decker Is

Potato

0   2   4
miles

Northeast Delta

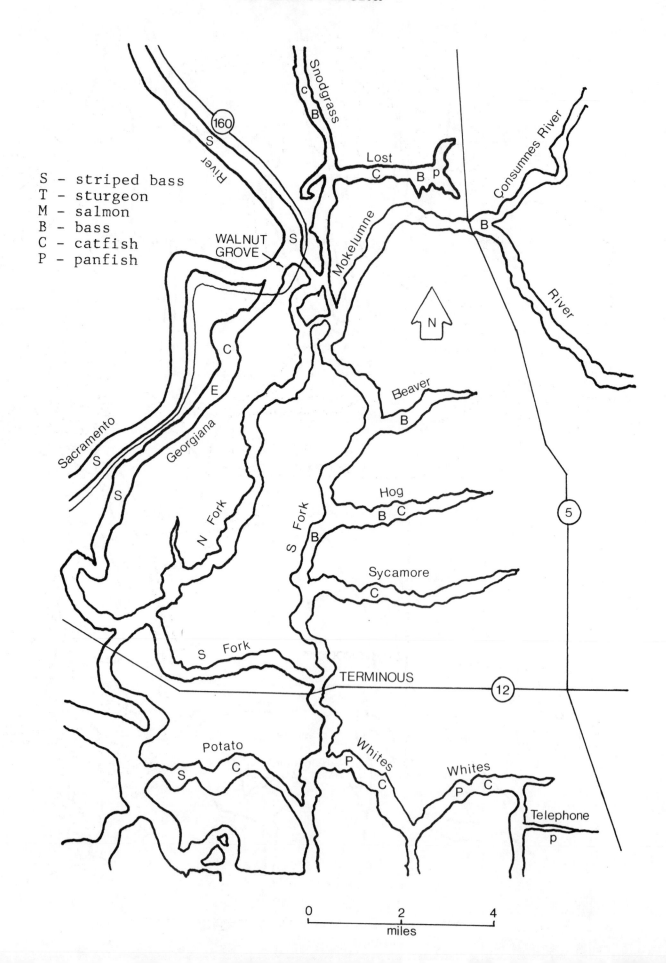

S — striped bass
T — sturgeon
M — salmon
B — bass
C — catfish
P — panfish

0   2   4
miles

Southwest Delta

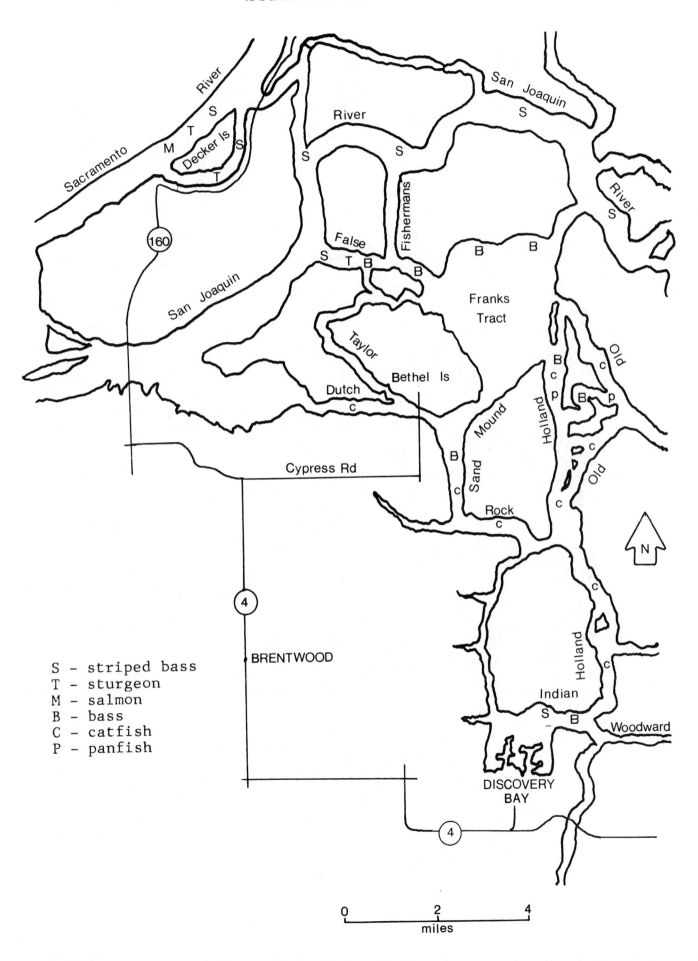

S – striped bass
T – sturgeon
M – salmon
B – bass
C – catfish
P – panfish

0   2   4
miles

Southeast Delta

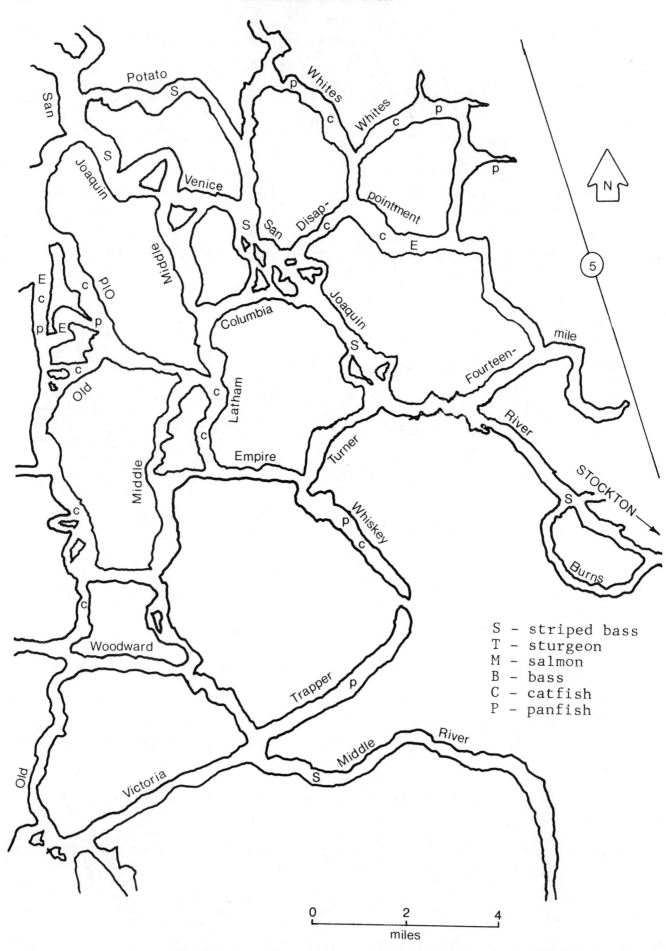

S – striped bass
T – sturgeon
M – salmon
B – bass
C – catfish
P – panfish

0   2   4
miles

Fish Cleaning

There's a syndrome among some anglers that I like to call, "The Fear of Filleting." It's not unlike "The Fear of Flying." But fortunately, it's a lot easier to overcome. It just takes a little knowledge, a little willingness, and an extra sharp filleting knife.

But, don't be mislead, filleting is not the end-all, or be-all of fish cleaning. It's only one of several basic approaches(all are presented here, in detail), and filleting is not even desirable or appropriate for some fish.

Field Dressing

Actually, the word dressing is not accurate, but we're stuck with it, so here goes. Field dressing means removing the entrails and gills of a fish just after catching. This process is generally reserved for large fish(several pounds or more). It's purpose is to preserve the fish at its height of freshness. Field dressing, for example, is quite common among ocean salmon anglers. It's the kind of thing that's desirable but not absolutely necessary. Especially if your catch is kept cold.

Here's how it's done. With the fish pointing away from you, put the tip of your knife in the anal vent and cut through the belly(leaving the intestines as undisturbed as possible) up to where the gills come together under the chin of the fish.

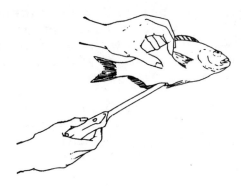

Next, with short cuts, free the bottom of the gills from the chin flesh and from the belly flesh.

 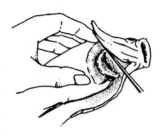

Now, pull open the gill cover on each side of the fish and cut the top of the gills free from the head. The gills and entrails can now be lifted or slid out of the fish in one unit. Now, finally, remove the strip of reddish tissue near the backbone in the intestinal cavity (this is the fishes kidneys). You may have to cut through a thin layer of tissue covering this area. As a last step, rinse off the fish. It is now ready for icing down.

Traditional Fish Cleaning

This approach is basically an extension of field dressing. As a young boy my earliest memory of fish cleaning was the assembly line my Dad set up with my brother and myself to clean a stringer of well over 100 Lake Michigan perch(about ½-1 pound each). Here are the steps;

1) Scaling - Using a knife(not necessarily real sharp) or a fish scaler, scrape from the tail towards the head. This is best done out-of-doors, since the scales fly around. Actually some fish(like salmon and sanddabs) can be

scaled with the spray from a garden hose nozzle. It's quick and easy.

2) Gutting - This is actually the same as the beginnings of field dressing. Open the belly from anal vent to gills.

3) Be-Heading - The entrails are slid forward and out of the body cavity, and then with a sharp knife, cut perpendicular to the backbone at the top of the gill cover, cut off the entrails, gills and head.

4) Rinsing - Rinse inside and outside of fish after removing red flesh in body cavity(see Field Dressing above).

5) Fish is now ready for cooking or preserving.

Filleting

Filleting is simple and has many advantages. For example, scaling is not necessary since the skin(and scales) will be removed. It can and often is done without even gutting or field dressing the fish first. It produces boneless or almost bone-free slabs of meat. And filleting works great on fish of all sizes and both round bodied and flat bodied fish.

Here are the steps in filleting;

1) Make the first cut just behind the gills. Cut down to the backbone, then turn the knife toward the tail of the fish and slice above the spine(feeling for it as you proceed) all the way to the tail. One flank of the fish will now be removed. Flip the fish over and repeat the process. This step is illustrated on the top of the next page.

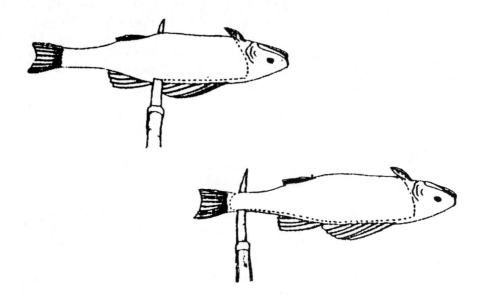

2) Now cut away the rib cage from each fillet. Inset the knife at the top of the rib cage and slice down following close to ribs.

3) Lastly, remove the skin. Lay fillet skin side down on cutting board. Insert the knife just about ½" from the tail and cut down to the skin. Now, firmly holding the tail-end, turn the blade forward and work the knife along the skin, "lifting" the meat from the skin all the way to the large end of the fillet.

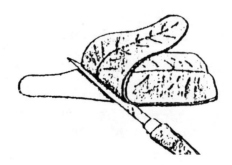

With a little practice, filleting becomes second nature. For a great visual display, watch the pros do it when a party boat docks after a day of fishing. You'll be amazed. Successful filleting depends on two things, once you understand the principles. One: use a good fish fillet knife. Two: keep the knife very sharp.

Steaking

Steaking simply means cutting a fish into similar-sized parts by making parallel cuts that are all perpendicular to the spine! Just joking! I know only math freaks and geometry teachers could understand that definition.

The first step in steaking(which, by the way, is usually reserved only for large fish) is to remove the head(this is done after field dressing), right at the gill cover. Now just lay the fish flat and divide it into about one inch thick pieces. The tail section(where the steaks are small) can be filleted. Some varieties need to be scaled before steaking.

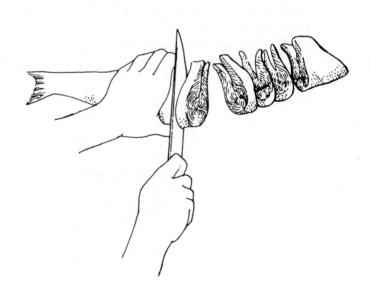

Keeping Fish Fresh

Fish is delicious. But it is also one of the most perishable of foods. So, from the time a fish is caught until it is served, care most be taken to preserve its freshness.

Freshness on the Water

If possible, the best way to keep a fish fresh, while continuing to fish, is to keep your catch alive. This can be done in several ways;

- For pan fish, use a collapsible basket. A fully submerged burlap bag also will serve the purpose.

- The best stringers are those that have large safety pin type clasps, and some type of swivel mechanism so fish are less likely to get twisted up.

- The proper stringing technique is to run the stringer through both the upper and lower lip. This allows the fish to open and close its mouth, thereby forcing water through its gills to breathe. Never run a stringer through the fishes gills. This prevents if from closing its mouth and therefore starving it of oxygen.

- Let out the full stringer. Even add a rope, if extra length is needed to keep the fish down deep in the water. The water is cooler and more oxygenated down deeper.

- If you move your boat quickly, lift stringer out of the water during a short trip.

- Surf and river anglers, who use a stringer, move the fish along with them, always placing them back into the deepest water available.

- When using a creel, bed and surround fish in dry grass. Canvas creels should be wet to maintain coolness.

There are some cautions to watch when keeping fish in water;

- Stringered fish have been known to have been eaten by turtles. Never string fish in warm water. Summertime surface water temperatures in some Northern California lakes are in the 80's!

- Stringers are taboo in salt waters. It's just feeding the sharks. Rather, use a cooler or fish-box, preferably with ice in it.

Freshness During Travel

If you're traveling for any length of time, follow these simple steps to insure freshness;

- Field dress the fish.

- Dry the fish thoroughly.

- Cover each fish with foil or plastic.

- Surround each package of fish, in a cooler, with crushed ice or cubed ice.

Refrigeration

Fish do not do particularly well under prolonged refrigeration. So it's best to either eat fresh caught fish, or freeze them. Refrigerated fish should be covered with heavy foil, freezer paper or plastic to prevent moisture from escaping.

Freezing

There are basically two ways to freeze fresh fish. With

either approach you can freeze whole-field cleaned fish, fish
fillets, steaks or chunks.

The first method is more conventional. Wrap fish in
packaging materials with high barriers to moisture and vapor
transmission. A good quality freezer wrapping paper or heavy
foil is recommended. Wrap tightly and tape securely. This
method is adequate. Better flavor and preservation can be
achieved by repeatedly dipping and freezing unwrapped fish
in water until a layer of ice is formed. Then wrap securely.

Actually, the best and simplest way to freeze fish is to
utilize old milk cartons, or similar liquid holding containers.
Fresh and well-cleaned fish can be placed in the container
up to an inch from the top. Now, simply fill the container
with water(or a brine solution of 1/3 cup of table salt to
one gallon of water) and shake to make sure there are no air
bubbles. Seal up container and freeze. Thawing is best done
on a drain rack so fish does not sit in cold water.

Cooking Fish

There are numerous fish cook books jam-packed with recipes. But, matching your favorite catch to an unfamiliar or inappropriate recipe often leads to less than enjoyable eating. Rather than special recipes, successful fish cooking depends on adhering to two simple principles;

1) Know when the fish is done-too often fish is over-cooked.

2) Match cooking method to the fish flavor, fish size and fat level.

First, let's address the "when fish is done" issue. Fish, by its very nature is more tender than red meat or poultry. It doesn't contain fibers that need to be broken down by extensive cooking. Some cooking experts say fish should be considered more like egg, than like meat. So, as in cooking egg, just enough heat need be applied to firm-up the protein. Over-cooking makes eggs tough and dry; it does the same for fish.

So how do you tell when fish is cooked for just the right length of time? It's easy. Fish is cooked properly when it flakes when probed with a fork. By flaking, I mean separated into its natural layers or divisions. This test should be done often, at the center, or thickest part of the fish fillet, steak, or whole fish.

Now, the second principle-matching the fish to the cooking method. First, some guidelines. Thin fillets (less than 5/8 inch) or small, whole fish are best for sauteing. Oily, or higher fat content fish are best for broiling, barbequing and baking. Lean fish are the easiest to poach. But, these guidelines have wide latitude. That's why, for each fish covered in this book, we give specific cooking preferences.

Sauteing

This method is often called frying, but frying is quite distinct. More on this in the pan frying section below. Sauteing is cooking fish in a frying pan, usually in a small amount of melted butter, over moderate or high heat.

This is one of the fastest and simplest ways to prepare fish. And, it is well-suited for either lean or fat fish. The fish is sprinkled with salt and pepper and dipped in flour on both sides. Cooking time per side varies from 1 minute to 3 minutes. A sauce can be prepared in the pan after the fish are removed to a warm platter.

Frying(both Pan and Deep)

Frying fish means emersing either partially or completely, in cooking oil. This process results in a thicker, more crusty covering of the fish than with sauteing or oven-frying. Frying usually involves a batter made with a beaten egg and a small amount of milk. The dipped fish pieces are rolled in bread crumbs, cracker crumbs or a purchased coating mix.

1/8 inch of shortening or salad oil should be heated to between 350° and 375° in a substantial frying pan. Or, if deep-frying, use enough shortening or salad oil in a deep fryer, to cover the fish. Heat to the same temperature. Finished fish should be golden brown and flake when tested.

Some pitfalls to avoid. Don't let the oil temperature fall. It results in a greasy or soggy coating. Too much fish put in the oil at one time can lower cooking temperature too much. Too high an oil temperature will result in dark coating or burnt flavor. If batter falls off, the fish pieces may have been too wet. So, pat dry before battering.

Oven Frying

Everybody knows how to oven-fry chicken, so everybody knows how to oven-fry fish. This method is simple and doesn't cause fat-spattering, if that's a problem with you.

Fish should be in serving-sized pieces. Dip each piece in milk, drain, sprinkle with salt and pepper, then roll in bread crumbs or cracker crumbs. Melt enough butter or margarine in a shallow baking pan to generously coat the bottom. Now, turn the crumb coated fish over in the melted butter or margarine and arrange the pieces in the pan. Bake in a hot oven(about 500°) until the fish flakes(from 5 to 15 minutes). Turn each piece one time so it browns evenly.

Baking

Foil wrapped or covered-dish oven cooking is the typical fish baking approach. The covering or enclosure is needed to prevent the fish from drying out. This is an ideal method for baking fish with vegetables, herbs or tomato sauce. The steam that is developed helps produce a tasty sauce. Oven temperature is usually about 450°.

Barbecuing or Grilling

Rich, full-flavored fish such as salmon, trout or albacore are most desirable for barbequing, since they're fatter and the smoke enhances the taste. Milder-tasting fish might be overcome by the smoke flavor. Serving-sized fillets, steaks and whole fish csn be barbequed.

Some people like to grill directly over the coals, while others put the fish on a sheet of heavy aluminum foil. The foil method works well in a covered grill because it prevents any sticking or turning problems.

Some helpful hints. Make sure the coals are hot and
the grill is hot. Fish stick like magnets to a cold grill.
Start fillets skin side up(if no foil is used) and turn only
once. If foil is used, fillet skin should be down(that is,
touching foil). While cooking, the fish is basted with melted butter or your favorite sauce.

Broiling

Broiling, of course, is much akin to barbecuing, except that the heat is above the fish. Any fish can be broiled, but leaner fish must be basted often to prevent it from
drying out. Fillets are often broiled on only one side,
while steaks are turned once. Broil 2-3 inches from the heat.

Poaching

Poaching is simmering fish gently in a flavorful liquid. The liquid is never boiled, however. Fish prepared
this way is very good served hot with a fish sauce made from
the poaching liquid. Any fish with a low fat content, and
salmon, of course, is delicious prepared this way. And, as
an extra bonus, cold, poached fish like albacore tuna or
salmon, is great.

Pieces of fish are often poached in cheese cloth while
large, whole fish are done in a poaching pan that has a special rack for lowering and removing the fish. Again, the
flake test will reveal when the fish is cooked properly.
Fillets should be tested after about 5 minutes.

Boiling

Boiling is a limited fish cooking technique. It is
only appropriate for rock crabs and crayfish, as described
in those sections.

Smoking

Many avid, and some not so avid, anglers own and use
fish smokers. They are simple to use and quite modestly
priced. And they produce delicious smoked fish. All commercially available smokers come with detailed instruction
manuals. It is also possible to convert such items as 55
gallon drums, or a discarded refrigerator and a hotplate.
Instructions for these do-it-yourself projects can be
found in smoking-oriented cook books in your local library.